# Essential
# Amsterdam

### by

### MICHAEL LEECH

Michael Leech is a travel writer and
contributes regularly to a
number of papers and magazines.
He has written books on
Italy and Washington.

**AA**

Produced by the Publishing Division of
The Automobile Association

Written by Michael Leech
Peace and Quiet Section
by Paul Sterry
Consultant: Frank Dawes

Edited, designed and produced by
the Publishing Division of The
Automobile Association.
Maps © The Automobile
Association 1990.

Distributed in the United Kingdom
by the Publishing Division of The
Automobile Association, Fanum
House, Basingstoke, Hampshire,
RG21 2EA.

A CIP catalogue record for this book
is available from the British Library.

ISBN 0 86145 869 9

Published by The Automobile
Association.

Typesetting: Avonset, Midsomer
Norton, Bath.
Colour separation: L C Repro,
Aldermaston.
Printing: S.R.L., Trento, Italy.

*Front cover picture:*
*The Keizersgracht at night*

This book employs a simple rating system to help choose which places to visit:

◆◆◆    do not miss

◆◆    see if you can

◆    worth seeing if you have time

## INTRODUCTION

*The picturesque canals and the houses that line them are a principal part of Amsterdam's attraction to visitors*

### INTRODUCTION

A thousand years ago Amsterdam was but a fishing village, out on the desolate marshes where two rivers met. The first settlers struggled to keep back the sea (an ever present danger to Holland) and created a dam on the Amstel river. So the name Amstel-Dam was born from that very first sea wall. Modern Amsterdam, large and lively, still has echoes of those early days and it keeps its feet and its feelings very close to water, for, of course, it is a city of canals. Do not be taken in by the banal travel brochure description of Amsterdam as 'the Venice of the North', however, for Amsterdam is anything but Venetian – it is as unique a city as its Belgian neighbour, Bruges, which is often saddled with a similar description. Amsterdam is no more like proud Venice than Venice is like Amsterdam – the city may have been built upon marsh and bog reclaimed from a greedy sea, but there the similarity ends. Amsterdam is uniquely itself, as much a product of trade and commercial aspirations as Venice is, yet quite different. It has an atmosphere and an air that travellers find heady and remarkable. It is a city that one always wants to get back to, however many times one has been there in the past.

**First Visits are Memorable**

Amsterdam is a city that extends a welcome, friendly and easy, to the visitor who has been there before, yet it also gives the first-timer a sense of pleasurable discovery allied with that same greeting. People come back surprised at the genial and kindly hospitality of the Dutch, their genuine pleasure in helping strangers and their unusually tolerant attitudes towards others whose tastes may not be their own. Amsterdam is in many ways a 'free city', a kind of San Francisco of Europe perhaps, a place where people can be themselves and do as they wish, and it is an ideal city for the young and those with a youthful attitude to living.

It has to be said that Amsterdam is a city where caution must be exercised, however, for toleration of drugs has made it attractive to cult followers and care should be taken when walking or driving in the city. This does not mean it is dangerous – merely that you should

*Amsterdam and much of the Netherlands are built on reclaimed land*

use common sense about valuables and locking car doors – a camera left in a car, an expensive handbag parked under a chair, can be a temptation in any city.

It is a walking city, so take comfortable, warm clothes and an umbrella, for like most of northern Europe, the city can be damp. Time and the 20th century have changed Amsterdam as much as most places, yet it still retains its character. Unlike its sister city, Rotterdam, which was almost flattened in World War II air-raids and which has risen like a phoenix in modern dress, Amsterdam has been spared for the most part the havoc of war. You can still find here an elegant city of the 17th and 18th centuries, gilded and glowing with period details, yet as lively and as innovative as ever in its attitudes today. It is a city of surprises, most of them delightful.

### Amsterdam Today

The present-day visitor will find a waterborne city of great beauty, with countless picturesque possibilities for photographers. It *is* crowded, there are many bicycles and pedestrians, bearing home the message that Holland is still the most tightly populated country in Europe and that many of the Dutch have chosen to live in Amsterdam! Despite the pressure of living, most Dutch people will pause to talk and they are particularly fond of their bars and clubs, where you will find them very much at home drinking beer, or Dutch gin, or cups of strong coffee. Try to talk to local people – you will find them voluble, proud of their homeland, and often very aware of the culture, history and background of Amsterdam in particular. It will give pleasure if you too reveal some knowledge of the city and its history. You are much helped, of course, in that most of Amsterdam's population will have some knowledge of European languages – many being quite fluent in English – and aware also that Dutch is not the easiest of tongues to master. Still, do try to acquire some words, and do not mind if the locals find it amusing at first! It is always gratifying to be able to say 'please' and 'thank you' in the language of your hosts.

*Amsterdam began life as a fishing village and has maintained the trade through the centuries*

## BACKGROUND

After the early beginnings of the village at the junction of the Amstel and the Ij rivers the settlement grew slowly, although it was soon to be recognised as an important focus for trade. Strategically placed, Amsterdam soon began to experiment with other business than mere fishing, and markets started up – before long the little village made itself a free port with special toll concessions, and this new attractiveness for commerce as a gateway from the North Sea to Europe caused growth over the neighbouring marshes and reclaimed land. As you stand on the grand central space before the Royal Palace known as the Dam Square you can reflect that somewhere under this paved space in the middle of Amsterdam must still lie the original dam. From here the city spread out in all directions, with building fed by the new affluence brought from abroad in a growing fleet of varied ships. Trade created the city; its solid hard-working merchants laid the foundations of its prosperity.

## The Arrival of the Canals

A major programme of development began for Amsterdam some four centuries ago when demand for increased docking space and new businesses created the right atmosphere for a new phase, the creation of the canals. They began, as so often with such schemes, in a small way, with the narrow straight canal along the Voorburgwal, close to the Dam, not much more than a moat, but opening the door for shipping to sail right into the city. After this initial success a plan evolved, and the ensuing waterways were created as a series of tightly curved crescents, enclosing the original straight canals. It is a unique plan, and if you look at the map you will see that Amsterdam is constructed on a series of U-shaped roads and canals, one inside the other, and all intended for easy access of shipping. Nowadays Amsterdam's canals may seem no more than sleepy backwaters, disturbed only by the occasional barge or tourist boat, but their origin was

completely commercial and if you could waft yourself back a couple of centuries you would see quite a different Amsterdam, with the canals crowded with shipping and the houses lining the canals all used for the new commerce. With these canals ships could dock right at their destinations and unload safely in the city centre. Look up at the gables

*Waterbuses carry visitors peacefully along canals that once bustled with the trading activities of wealthy merchants*

of Amsterdam, and you will often see the hoists and supports for cranes sticking out. These are still used today, for the canal houses are tight on interior space and large items of furniture sometimes have to be swung into the houses on ropes and pulleys, through the suitably large windows. These houses were all once storehouses and workshops, upper floors buzzing with activities and merchants living, this time, 'under the shop'.

The canals were limited to four major interior ones (one linked to the river's path out towards the increasingly distant sea) and a girdling one that neatly belts in the old city in its more loosely curved path – the Singel. The River Amstel runs across these canals and is much broader and more impressive as it flows down to the Oude Schans and the docks. Within the old city, and also in the suburbs, are other canals connected to the central system. Most of them will have roads and paths beside them, so they can easily be seen by the pedestrian; although the major ones are cluttered with cars there is a good deal of traffic-free space in the heart of the city.

**Foreign Domination**
In the 16th century the great empire built up by a conquering Spain, rich on its trade with the Indies, began to crumble. The Spanish had long held the Netherlands and the 'Low Countries', trying forcibly to crush the deeply felt Protestantism of the Dutch and enforcing many indignities on the local population. At last, in 1609, the once powerful Spanish were obliged to make a truce with the rebellious Dutch, and this led slowly yet inevitably to a withdrawal which was effected by 1648. At last, after many struggles and fights for independence, the provinces of the Netherlands were finally free from foreign domination. With a great surge of confidence the newly released provinces embarked

# BACKGROUND

*The city has a rich architectural inheritance left by prosperous merchant classes*

on a period of development and expansion now known as the Golden Age – and Amsterdam was its centre and its spark. A fresh vitality swept through the country, an era of exploration and new trade was launched as far-off countries were drawn into Amsterdam's influence, and concurrent with this came a glorious encouragement of culture and the arts. Museums in Amsterdam and abroad show this new confidence in paintings, sculpture, gold and silver ware, porcelain, fabrics and furnishings, a bursting

desire to tap held-down energies and make the new nation splendid in every way. It was a rarity too, for the men and women who were directing those expressions of pride and new strength were not aristocrats but business people who had been brought up on trade. Unlike most other European capitals, where top society was basically one of noble birth, Amsterdam's leaders were of the merchant classes and they brought a new force to this surge of activity, and it is their Amsterdam that we see when exploring the city now – the canal houses, as they are called, in which these merchants lived and worked line the waterways, tightly packed together, a splendid parade of fine architecture that is very much a Dutch development.

## Royal Connections

Amsterdam has always had a royal palace, although it is no longer used as a residence (the Queen now lives in The Hague). Three hundred years ago William of Orange was called over to England, having married James II's daughter in 1677, to reign jointly there as William and Mary from 1689 to 1694. The line ended when there were no heirs, and for the following century Holland alternated between being a monarchy and a republic, eventually gaining its present shape in 1830 when modern Belgium was formed.

## The Twentieth Century

Holland remained neutral during World War I, but in World War II the country was invaded by Germany and during this terrible time many Dutch people were deported, including most of the large Jewish population that had made the city their home. Despite much protest from their neighbours and friends these citizens of Amsterdam were taken to slave labour and concentration camps, never to return. Anne Frank's diary drew the world's attention to the plight of a typical Jewish family during these years, and her house and the famous attic hiding place is much visited (see page 26). Throughout Amsterdam there are monuments to the citizens who went into Nazi Germany to imprisonment and death at this time. Amsterdam, besides being a modern, pragmatic city with liberal attitudes, does not forget the past and the dreadful war years of 1939 to 1945 when many of its citizens faced censure for making public protests about the deportations.

Amsterdam has grown considerably during the past four decades, with suburbs extending across the flat lands around the city to make it a major European conurbation, and it has added amenities and modernised others. Schiphol is a well-planned

## BACKGROUND

airport, the headquarters of the national airline KLM Royal Dutch Airlines, and it is placed conveniently close to not only Amsterdam but also The Hague and other big centres. (Although Amsterdam is the nation's capital the government meets in The Hague.) There are new connections by road and rail to other European cities, and the capital is well served with motorways (which are toll free). Trains are particularly well-run in this country, and you can get swiftly and easily to all parts of Holland in quicker time than it takes to drive. There is a system of streetcars or trams in the city, easy to operate on zoned tickets which give you a specific time to make your journey and allow for changes, and there is also a new subway system. Many of the citizens use bicycles and you can rent a bike at the central railway station or at other centres. There are, of course, taxi services too, but with the narrow streets of the old city often much congested you are often better advised to use public transport or to walk. The centre is compact and easy to understand once you have orientated yourself. Amsterdam is a busy commerical centre still, with a wealth of businesses from cut flowers to diamonds, and tourism is a major earner of money, too. There are many hotels in all categories, numerous places to visit, and good shopping. Holland is a leading member of the European Economic Community and has benefited greatly from membership of the Common Market. Most Dutch people are ardently pro European, recognising its advantages while realising that closer relationships with other nations have in no way changed or spoiled a cherished way of life. Residents of this city by the sea are proud of their citizenship, and while at times Amsterdam may seem to be groaning at its seams, with crowds of visitors and business people adding to the stresses, there are always quiet places in this ancient port and principal town where you can look on views unchanged in centuries and smell the ocean on the damp breezes, reminding you that Amsterdam's friend, enemy and ally all in one is never far away.

### What you will Find in Amsterdam Today

You can spend many hours in Amsterdam wandering along the canals, admiring the canal houses, monuments of another age – all similar in size and shape and all different, particularly the gables, many of which are elaborately plastered with scrolls and flutings, a kind of exuberant flourish above the suitably sober façades. These houses are now much sought after as residences in the central city, and many are divided into flats. They are strictly controlled by the city, and changes may not be made to the brown brick fronts, nor to the elaborate doorways which are often approached by flights of stone steps. They make a good photograph, especially if reflected in a canal.

The original plan of Amsterdam is much the same today, even with modern accretions and some high-rise building. (Under the streets of Amsterdam are many

*The bicycle is a staple means of transport for the locals, but an efficient tram system also operates in the city*

thousands of log piles driven into the mud to make firm foundations for buildings more than a very few storeys high. It is not surprising, therefore, that the tallest ones in Amsterdam are still church towers.)

The central axis of the city has the main rail station at one end and the Muntplein at the other with the oldest canals running parallel to the line of the Damrak and the Rokin, the two central thoroughfares that effectively cut the old centre in half. To the east of this line is an ancient quarter of old streets with two canals along the Oudezijds Voorburgwal (normally written OZ Voorburgwal) and the Oudezijds Achterburgwal (OZ Achterburgwal). The Kloveniersburgwal with its canal effectively closes this quarter and beyond it to the east along the Jodenbreestraat is the old Jewish quarter and the Artis Zoo. South of the old centre and across the arms of the Amstel river is the Rembrandtsplein with its bars and clubs and local restaurants. Next, going clockwise, is the Leidseplein with its lively street life and hotels and across the Singelgracht is the museum area with many of its streets named after Dutch artists. The city continues its sweep from the Leidsestraat along the four central U-shaped canals up to the railway lines along the Ij river with a fascinating old quarter, the Jordaan, slipped in between the Prinsengracht and the Marnixstraat at the northwestern end. Eastwards from these last areas is the central Dam Square, with its impressive church and the classical façade of the Royal Palace. Giving onto the Dam is the principal shopping street, the pedestrian-only thoroughfare known as the Kalverstraat. Close by is the famous Red Light District which you can walk through with perfect safety – providing you do not irritate the 'girls'! Near by in the many small streets are numerous bars, often open late at night and

*Merchants decorated the façades of their houses with elaborate gables and doorways, often using symbols of their name or trade*

catering for a range of tastes, bringing in thousands of Dutch people and foreign visitors every night. Almost everything is available in Amsterdam and the sex-bars are famous, but you are politely warned not to the industry is carefully controlled and there is no evidence of violence and crime as a rule in the well-delineated sex sections.

## The People of Amsterdam

People make places and that is as true of Amsterdam as anywhere. The elegance and style of Amsterdam was laid down centuries ago by its proud business people. The fact that this is a city which had to be fought for and defended inclines the Dutch to an impressive passion for liberty and the rights of the individual. The city is an unusual place, even for Europe where many other cities are characterised by forceful residents – one thinks of the elegant women of Paris, of the style and poise of the Romans, of the solid grey business men of Zürich all contributing to the image of their cities. The conventional idea of a Dutch person is of a straightforward, bluff, easy-going individual of liberal mind – and that's not far off, yet there is a lot more to the Dutch than that, and in a way the residents of Amsterdam can be as different from other Dutchmen as a New Yorker is from a Middle-Westerner. The complex Amsterdam character is reflected in a hundred ways in this waterborne city, yet a few kilometres away in the countryside are communities that surprise with their bigotry and domination by a narrow religious cult. The citizen of Amsterdam has seen a lot of life and, since everything is more than usually 'close up' in

go in if they are likely to offend you. 'Live and let live' is the Amsterdam motto, and it certainly has been good for business! (For addresses and recommendations see Amsterdam by Night, pages 102-4.) The wide windows in which the girls sit with their attractions well displayed are a feature of Amsterdam, yet

## BACKGROUND

this crowded city, he or she tends to be of philosophic bent and quite ready to live and let live. Amsterdam is an unusually 'laid back' city and it also has a very large population of young people; in its scattered university and in its appeal to the youth of other nations it has gathered many young people into its confines and their presence adds a note of lightness and freedom to the city.

The 'live and let live' philosophy extends to sex and allows a flourishing of sex shops and allied businesses such as cinemas and exhibitions, bookshops and video-centres. Usually bathed in neon glare or pink suffused lighting, these establishments can be found all over the city and rarely get more than a shrug of the shoulder from resident and visitor alike. The

*Numerous restaurants, bars and clubs make for a lively street life in parts of the city*

attitude also accounts for the fact that homosexual bars and clubs are common and the city has become a magnet for weekend visitors from Germany, France and the UK to drink and dance in the late-night bars of the old quarter or beside the Leidseplein.

As a stranger, walking in Amsterdam, you often come across an example of welcoming warmth and pleasant smiles, unusual for a big city. The overall

impression from shop assistant to bus driver is of an obliging friendliness and interest. People in general seem eager to help, to give you directions, or just to exchange a word of greeting.

On the other hand, Holland is a very densely occupied country with a large number of people filling up the roughly 200 by 100 miles (320km by 160km) country, and at times you do sense an aggressiveness and a need to assert one's 'space'. It is not likely that the short-time visitor will see this side of the Amsterdam character, yet people who have lived for periods of time there tell of rudeness and even minor violence towards each other and a need from time to time to show one is not being pushed down by the sheer weight of people.

Amsterdam must be the only 'foreign' city where English is so universally spoken, with up to 70 per cent of the population having a working knowledge of the language, and where you can get around almost without a word of Dutch. English is a major subject in schools, and the people learn it because it is an international tongue and often necessary to work and leisure. Also Dutch is hard for a foreigner to pronounce with its hard nasal quality and curious twisted sounds that seem to make the tongue do acrobatics in the mouth. This fluency in English is of course somewhat embarrassing to a visitor who has laboriously learned a few words of Dutch, and it also

*Proud householders indulge the national passion for flowers*

means that in Amsterdam it is hard to practise the local language since most residents will at once obligingly turn to the English language when they realise that is your native tongue. In addition many Dutch people have visited other European countries and their knowledge of foreign places and customs can be surprising. The warmth and interest of the people of Amsterdam makes it

an ideal first time place for someone who has not travelled much, for assistance is readily forthcoming in shops and on the street. There is a touch of curiosity often expressed too, for Amsterdammers like to know where visitors have come from and what their impressions are of Holland. The Dutch are polite, but they are certainly not shy.

The people of Amsterdam have decided facial and physical characteristics, being strongly built with big bones and solid bodies. Faces are often bold and even craggy, eyes usually blue or grey and features well-determined. Blond hair predominates, and men will often have moustaches. The young are athletic and well developed, well fed and healthy and they tend to dress fashionably and casually. Children are charming – and beautifully cared for with smart hair styles and modish clothes. Much of the city is geared for children, and family outings to the parks and museums are common, especially at weekends.

The people of Amsterdam are difficult to generalise upon, yet the visitor will find them casual, cultivated and easy-going, and they add immensely to one's enjoyment of their city since they seem to be quite happy that you want to come and share it with them for a time. It is well worth while trying to make some friends in this engaging town and organisations do exist for putting people in touch with the Dutch so if you would like closer links then enquire at the Netherlands Board of Tourism. Drop any natural reserve you may have about talking to strangers, and aim to strike up conversations and discussions – there are numerous cafés and 'brown bars' and even in the trains and the buses people can be quite talkative.

**Where they Live**

As you come in from the ports by road, or on a train, or by airport bus or taxi, you will pass through extensive suburbs on the way into the centre and this is where the mass of Amsterdammers live in low-rise flats and small houses, neatly framed in lawns and flower beds with water never far away. The suburbs are in general well planned and airy with trees and wide roads, yet there is an overall air of blandness which can be grey and almost grim in winter days when the sky is filled with lowering clouds. Many residents will commute into central Amsterdam to work using the new Metro lines (two of them), buses and bicycles, but rarely cars, for the city is crammed and car parking is very limited. (Illegally parked vehicles are ticketed and often clamped. These areas are marked with warning signs in several languages.) Cars are ranked tightly all along the canal sides where there is room, and the occasional plunge into a canal by someone who isn't adept at stopping in time is not unusual! Fortunately the water is not deep and a marooned vehicle is easily dragged out of the mud by a special city crane truck.

In the centre people live on all floors of the houses and a flat in a canal house is highly desirable. It is not a Dutch habit to curtain windows so you will see right into interiors, often veiled simply with net draperies, and particularly at night you will get a feeling of looking into a painting with the beams, decorations and sculpted ceilings of the old houses glimpsed from below. Windows are very large to capture all the northern light and doors are functional. Inside entry spaces are narrow and stairs as steep as it is possible to imagine them – all this to take up as small a space as possible and to allow more room for living. This concern with space is evident in all sorts of ways in Amsterdam. Look at the roof-lines of the houses: even they are steeply raked and high and a flat roof is a rarity. Behind the houses in the centre you may find tiny gardens and courtyards with tubs and trees – almost Japanese in the careful concern with maximum use of limited space. These are usually hard to see from outside, although exploration of little streets and alleys off the main thoroughfares may reward you with glimpses. An unusual and very pretty formal garden with box-edged parterres and espalier-like trees may be seen off the main Amstelstraat opposite the entrance to Wagenstraat. This is quite a large garden for Amsterdam and is actually part of a museum on the Herengracht (see under Willet-Holthuysen Museum, page 32). It dates from the 18th century and is fenced from the busy Amstelstraat with a high iron railed grille.

The Dutch, not surprisingly, are mad for plants and flowers and use every cranny and shelf to put pots on both inside and outside houses, while even in the city centre some houses are draped with ivies and other creepers making whole streets resemble something in the country. It is well worthwhile taking a stroll along the flower market on the Singel where pot plants and flowers spread across the pavements for a long block, with covered premises behind. (See Flower Market under What to see, page 35.)

Pots of flowers even perch on the many canal boats where people have taken to the water in order to live. Some canals are quite cluttered with boats moored against the sides and some are so constructed that they look more like floating houses than rivercraft. Most of the houseboats will never move, but occasionally you can see one being manoeuvred into a space. Cats and dogs promenade the decks, birdcages hang in windows, laundry dries on makeshift lines and it all looks rather gipsy-like and casual. No doubt there are many problems in living close to the water-line yet these floating homes are neat and comfortable inside, with space most carefully conserved of course, and they can be quite palatial with all amenities and often a wood-burning stove poking its snout of a chimney above the cabin line.

A few people live on the streets of the city but, apart from the drifting 'druggies', street people are not as obvious as in other major cities such as Paris and London where the floating population seems to be getting bigger all the time.

## WHAT TO SEE

### Introduction

In its relatively small space Amsterdam has many attractions, but one that regularly brings in visitors from all over the world is the array of museums to be found here. Some of the most famous paintings in the world cluster in Amsterdam and other Dutch cities, from Vermeer to Rembrandt, from Rubens to Ruisdael, with a whole modern building devoted to the works of van Gogh. You could spend a week in Amsterdam and not see all its galleries – nor would you be well advised to, since there is such a plenitude of fine things that any reasonable viewer would find it all too much. Take time and plan visits carefully to avoid the fatigue of overstretching yourself: there *is* an enormous amount to see, but there is no point in spoiling a visit with overkill.

*The Rijksmuseum, one of the world's greatest art galleries*

## WHAT TO SEE – INTRODUCTION

Most galleries demand a fee for entrance of around 3 or 4 guilders, but if you are planning several museum visits you would be well advised to buy a **Museumcard** (**Museumjaarkart**) at a set price which will provide you with entry not just for the few days you may be there, but for a calendar year. Buy it at participating places or from the VVV Amsterdam Tourist Office in Stationsplein or Leidsestraat. Some museums do not honour this card but it is always stated at the entry along with the times of opening and prices.

There is a very useful canal boat service that makes stops close to museums. The **Museumboat** is operated with the Touristram and its schedule is such that if you plan carefully you can go to individual museums and at the end of your visit the next boat will be waiting to take you onwards. The flat fee for the boat for a day (about 5 guilders) also includes some other services such as the guide (if you know what you want to see you will not find this of much interest as it is only a generalised introduction) and reductions in admission fees at the museums *en route*. A summer service.

The golden age provided the impetus for Dutch art to break into a bloom as glorious as the tulip fields in spring. The new ideas and commercial ventures of the 17th century, when many businesses were born in Amsterdam, created a flow of money and then a demand for beautiful objects to adorn the new houses. In other countries this might have resulted in so many conventional overpainted and gilded depictions of classical, mythical or religious subjects, but while these were occasionally present the individuality of Dutch art of that time is what intrigues and charms, for a new style had been born. In much of Europe at the time a tide of baroque art was sweeping through palaces and churches – still to be seen in Italy, Germany and Spain in a welter of plasterwork and paint – but in the Low Countries there was a different system of patronage. It was not great churchmen and imperious aristocrats who were demanding art; this time it was the newly rich bourgeois and they wanted something different. Pictures and statues were not encouraged in the Protestant churches, so there was no outlet there, but that left the artists free to work for individuals who demanded no set style. Instead of drooping madonnas, flights of angels and sweeps of foliage and feathers set in ostentatious frames or architectural conceits designed for palaces and cathedrals, we get smaller, more compact canvases, suitable for hanging in Amsterdam rooms, their subjects the life of the people who lived and worked in these settings, or still-life pictures, or unostentatious portraits. For the first time in European history, genre paintings came *van Gogh's Seascape, 1888, one of many oils and drawings in the Vincent van Gogh Museum*

on the scene, and were produced in their thousands. There are many examples of the new and eye-opening works in the major Rijksmuseum, room upon room of them in fact, but you can also see contemporary pictures in more modest places giving you an impression of how they looked in their 17th-century settings. It is interesting that the trade and industry flourishing in Amsterdam at the time produced so many artists, and some of them world masters whose work continues to be of enormous interest.

Rembrandt's sombre and thoughtful canvases spring to mind, and certainly he is one of Amsterdam's most famous sons with many of his works owing their inspiration to the city and its life. Vermeer of Delft is a mystery man, for there are only a handful of his pictures in existence and these take pride of place in world museums from London's National Gallery to New York's Metropolitan Museum. His detailed paintings of domestic interiors are noted for their purity, their richness of colour and their treatment of daylight tones.

The works of the 17th century supply a clue about the Dutch character today, indicating tastes and values that still remain basic. Perhaps an unsuspected trait is revealed in the renegade artist, Vincent van Gogh, who lived in the

## WHAT TO SEE – INTRODUCTION

second half of the 19th century and belonged to the Post-Impressionists. The Vincent van Gogh Museum is a must for anyone interested in the development of modern art, and here you can see hundreds of oils and drawings originally owned by his brother.

The 17th century also had an indelible effect on the other arts, and at the Rijksmuseum are many galleries of silver, porcelain, sculpture, tapestries, ivories, jewellery and furniture – another good reason for making a second or even a third visit, for these galleries are very extensive and present prime examples of works by leading artists and humble craftsmen. Examples can also be seen in such smaller museums as the Willet-Holthuysen Museum (a canal house restored to period opulence) and the Amsterdam Historisch Museum which contains a range of artefacts and objects depicting the city's power and prestige as it grew. In Rembrandthuis you get a strong feeling of what this city house was like when in his early and prosperous years the artist lived here, opposite the wide waters of the Oude Schans.

Modern and contemporary art can be found at the modern Stedelijk Museum, not far from the Rijksmuseum and the van Gogh Museum. Artists of the last one hundred years, principally, are represented including Chagall, Picasso, van Gogh, and the French Impressionists. Material also

*The city's story as told in the Amsterdams Historisch Museum*

includes sculpture, graphic art, industrial design, posters, pop art, etc.

### Museums

The *Museum Card (Museumjaarkart)*, available from the VVV Amsterdam Tourist Office and participating museums and valid for one calendar year (half-price for under 25's), gives free admission to 18 museums in Amsterdam and more than 300 others around the country.

*Open*: Tuesday to Friday 10.00 to 17.00; Saturday, Sunday, festive days 13.00 to 17.00
*Closed*: Monday; 1 January, 30 April

◆
### AMSTELKRING MUSEUM ('OUR LORD IN THE ATTIC')
*Oude Zijds Voorburgwal 40*
Hidden Catholic church in the attics of canal houses plus furnished part of 17th-century house. This is very much a surprise museum – tiny, yet fascinating, and the attic church is amazingly elaborate. It really couldn't have been a complete secret when it was built because local people must have been aware of people entering the house.
*Open*: Monday to Saturday 10.00 to 17.00; Sunday, festive days 13.00 to 17.00
*Closed*: 1 January

◆◆
### AMSTERDAMS HISTORISCH MUSEUM
*Kalverstraat 92*
Amsterdam's past in models, sculptures, paintings and photographs set in the former City Orphanage beside the Begijnhof.
*Open*: Daily 11.00 to 17.00
*Closed*: 1 January

◆
### ALLARD PIERSON MUSEUM
*Oude Turfmarkt 127*
Archaeological museum with collection of the University of Amsterdam; Egypt, Asia Minor, Greece. A series of small, intimate galleries crowded with well-displayed pottery, metalwork, sculpture, jewellery, fabrics and small dioramas of ancient events such as athletic events in classical Greece. All listings seem to be in Dutch, although there is a brief and not very satisfactory English guide.

◆
### AMSTERDAM SEX MUSEUM
*Damrak 18*
This is really an attempt to make the rather lurid sex life of Amsterdam into something 'respectable', but basically it is a place for people to go in and have a laugh (often embarrassed). A sort of dig-in-the-ribs gallery showing 18th-

## WHAT TO SEE – MUSEUMS

and 19th-century pictures and statues and modern attitudes. Probably provides a service for those who don't dare to go into nearby sex shops.

### ◆◆◆ ANNE FRANKHUIS
*Prinsengracht 263*
The top floor, well hidden, is famous as the cramped World War II hiding place of the Frank family, who managed to spend many months here in close confinement, their life recorded by the diligent Anne. Her diary was left quite by chance, giving us her vivid views of their 'internal exile'. The experiences and touching revelations of this young Jewish girl are still moving. In addition there are regularly changing presentations of all forms of racism.
*Open*: Monday to Saturday 09.00 to 17.00; Sunday, festive days 10.00 to 17.00; June to August open until 19.00
*Closed*: 25 December, 1 January, Yom Kippur

### ◆◆ AVIODROME
*Schiphol Centrum*
National air travel museum with all sorts of flying machines from antique aircraft to space vehicles. Train from Central Station.
*Open*: Daily 10.00 to 17.00
*Closed*: Monday, 1 November to 1 April; 25 and 31 December, 1 January

### ◆ BIJBELS MUSEUM
*Herengracht 366*
Here there is a chance to see the interiors of two canal

houses turned into a museum of bibles. Do not be put off – it is a lively and inventive museum with interesting interiors and children will enjoy it. The interiors are worth noting for their period details.
*Open*: Tuesday to Saturday 10.00 to 17.00; Sunday, festive days 13.00 to 17.00
*Closed*: Monday; 1 January, 30 April, 1 May

### ◆ BOSMUSEUM
*Amsterdamse Bos*
A forest of deciduous woodland, this 'wood museum' is like a park, but the information centre has exhibits

on aspects of this unusual man-made preserve.
*Open*: Daily 10.00 to 17.00

◆
**CHILDREN'S MUSEUM**
*Linnaeusstraat 2*
See page 111

◆◆
**CIVIC GUARD GALLERY**
*off the Kalverstraat*
Part of the Amsterdam Historisch Museum (see above), this is a beautifully designed passage with displays and paintings to illustrate the life of the Amsterdam guilds and guards of earlier centuries. The arcade is a public passage and entry is free. Views beyond the glass give onto peaceful old houses, making a handsome backdrop to exhibits.

◆
**FODOR MUSEUM**
*Keizersgracht 609*
Contemporary work by Dutch artists.
*Open*: Daily 11.00 to 17.00
*Closed*: 1 January

◆◆
**JOODS HISTORISCH MUSEUM**
*Jonas Daniel Meijerplein 2–4*
This is a major museum and will be of interest to anyone

*A fine collection of holy Jewish objects on display in the Joods Historisch Museum*

with a mind to learn, Jewish or not. It has been converted from an old synagogue and contains well-displayed items ranging from works of Jewish artists to all sorts of objects from home and religious life. It stands in the old Jewish quarter, and its collection, once housed in the Waag or Weigh-house, is extensive.
*Open*: Daily 11.00 to 17.00
*Closed*: Yom Kippur

◆◆
### 'T KROMHOUT MUSEUM
*Hoogte Kadijk 147*
This 'werfmuseum' is actually a quay where steamships and other historic ships are constructed and repaired.

*The Rijksmuseum houses a vast collection of art and artefacts. Above: stained glass window*

*Open*: Monday to Friday 10.00 to 16.00
*Closed*: Saturdays, Sundays, festive days

◆
### MADAME TUSSAUD'S WAX MUSEUM
*Kalverstraat 156*
See pages 110-11
*Open*: Daily 10.00 to 18.00; July, August until 19.00
*Closed*: 25 December

◆
### NETHERLANDS FILMMUSEUM
*Vondel Park 3*
Exhibition of cameras and

photographic equipment
*Open*: Tuesday to Friday 10.00
to 17.00
*Closed*: Saturday to Monday

◆
### OVERHOLLAND MUSEUM
*Museumplein 4*
Paper works (drawings,
posters, collages) by modern
Dutch artists with some other
countries also represented.
*Open*: Tuesday to Saturday
11.00 to 17.00; Sunday, festive
days 13.00 to 17.00
*Closed*: Monday; 25
December, 1 January, 30 April

◆◆
### REMBRANDTHUIS MUSEUM
*Jodenbreestraat 4–6*
When Rembrandt was young
and prosperous, with many
commissions and pupils to
teach, he acquired this large
house to suit his new-found
respectability and income.
Later he became
impoverished, but at this time
of his busy life he was well-off.
It is a cheerful house with a
view – its gaily coloured
shutters and banners proclaim
it from a distance. Works on
show include 250 etchings.
*Open*: Monday to Saturday
10.00 to 17.00; Sunday, festive
days 13.00 to 17.00
*Closed*: 1 January

◆◆◆
### RIJKSMUSEUM
*Stadhouderskade 42*
This vast art collection is one
no visitor to Amsterdam should
miss, even if ideally you
should make several visits
(another reason for acquiring a
museum card for unlimited
entries). The building looks a
bit like a palace, although it
was always intended as a
museum and has all the marks
of 19th-century respect for high
art – and that indeed is what
you will find once beyond the
ornate towers. It is not just a
picture gallery, even with its
colossal collection. It is the
national museum as its name
implies and within, in a maze of
galleries, are rooms dedicated
to the crafts of the country –
from dishes to doll's houses,
from silverware to tapestries
and a special section tying into
the country's colonial past with
East India artefacts. There are
three levels to this huge
repository; start with a guide
book from the desk in the
central hall and take time
deciding what you want to see.
The paintings, in a warren of
large high-ceilinged galleries,
go from 15th-century to 19th-
century works and include
famous examples such as the
paintings of Vermeer of Delft.
This mystery man left very few
canvases and these take pride
of place in leading world
collections – there are several
here indicating his uncanny
ability to encompass the
felicity of calm and repose in
colours that seem touched with
an unearthly glow – note
particularly the blues and the
golden-browns. Emotion is
suppressed in these canvases
and ordinary people going
about everyday tasks achieve
a quality of timelessness. *The
Night Watch* by Rembrandt is
a favourite in its own room but
there are many other fine
examples of Dutch and
Flemish art to enjoy.

There is a good café here, but like those in many museums in Holland it is not cheap.
*Open*: Tuesday to Saturday 10.00 to 17.00; Sunday, festive days 13.00 to 17.00
*Closed*: Monday; 1 January

◆◆
### SCHEEPVAART MUSEUM
*Kattenburger Plein 1*
The Netherlands Maritime Museum is contained in the former armoury of the Admiralty. History of Dutch navigation, ship models.
*Open*: Tuesday to Saturday 10.00 to 17.00; Sunday, festive days 13.00 to 17.00
*Closed*: Monday; 1 January

◆
### SIX COLLECTION
*Amstel 218*
The Six Collectie as it is called locally is a private gathering of works of art of the 17th century, taking its name from the Six family whose head was Jan Six. This collector is pictured by Rembrandt, whose friend he was, in a major portrait in this small yet very impressive collection of paintings. (Unfortunately you cannot just wander in off the street – you need to make a special reservation by contacting the Rijksmuseum and requesting a visiting card.)

◆◆
### STEDELIJK MUSEUM
*Paulus Potterstraat 13*
Amsterdam's major collection of modern art from 1850 on, shown in a series of large rooms, in a gallery in the same area as the Rijksmuseum and the van Gogh Museum. Here

there is a great choice of Dutch and French art of the last one hundred years principally, with examples of Chagall, Picasso, van Gogh, and the French Impressionists predominating, but there are also vast rooms of abstract, surrealist, experimental works. In addition there are often special shows at the Stedelijk as well as film-shows and concerts (quite common in Amsterdam's galleries), lectures and theatrical presentations. The collection, which is indeed a huge one, also features photography, posters, prints, graphics, and a range of new works involving many elements. Sculpture too, but then that can be seen everywhere in Amsterdam,

and modern design for business and industry is also featured. Early Dutch works are fascinating since they are often little-known outside this country, and these alone can provide an excuse for a long visit. There is a library and of course you can buy reproductions of works you enjoy.
*Open*: Daily 11.00 to 17.00
*Closed*: 1 January

### ◆ THEATRE INSTITUTE
*Herengracht 166*
The Nederlands T I gives a history of Dutch theatre.
*Open*: Tuesday to Sunday, festive days 11.00 to 17.00

**Wheatfield**, *painted by van Gogh in 1888, towards the end of his life*

*Closed*: Monday; 25 December, 1 January, 30 April, 1 May

### ◆◆ TROPENMUSEUM
*Linnaeusstraat 2*
Cultures and lives of Third World peoples, well-presented displays with sub-tropical environments, artefacts, ecology.
*Open*: 10.00 to 17.00 weekdays; Saturday, Sunday, festive days 12.00 to 17.00
*Closed*: 1 January, 30 April, 5 May

### ◆ VAN LOON MUSEUM
*Vijzelstraat 672*
Canal house preserved in original state. Van Loon family antiques. Portraits.
*Open*: Monday only

### ◆◆◆ VINCENT VAN GOGH MUSEUM
*Paulus Potterstraat 7*
A modern museum impressively designed for the pictures of the 19th-century artist, part of the Rijksmuseum. 200 paintings and 500 drawings depict his progress and there are also the Japanese prints he worked from. His paintings now command such colossal prices on world markets as to seem almost obscene, especially when they are destined for bank vaults as money-appreciating investments. Vincent lived a lonely and troubled life. After a quarrel with Gauguin he cut off his ear in remorse and was put into an asylum. Shortly after, at the age of 37, he committed

## WHAT TO SEE – MUSEUMS

suicide, leaving behind a mass of works, many painted in the south of France. The collection includes hundreds of drawings and paintings owned by his devoted brother Theo. You enter the museum and trace the painter's career in a dramatic progress from early experiments to the final fiercely coloured, troubled works.

*Open*: Tuesday to Saturday 10.00 to 17.00; Sunday, festive days 13.00 to 17.00
*Closed*: Monday; 1 January

### ◆◆
### WILLET-HOLTHUYSEN MUSEUM
*Herengracht 605*
A meticulously furnished canal house showing the luxurious life of 17th–18th-century burghers. The family was wealthy and socially prominent in 17th-century Amsterdam and the house was built in 1687 to show the riches and possessions of the family as much as to be lived in, it seems. Here you can see wide-ranging collections of porcelain, antique pottery, high quality Dutch furniture and silver, also glass and carpets and, inevitably, more pictures! But the house itself is a perfect foil, and the rooms are exquisite with much carved wood and marble, and painted ceilings too. It is also very well kept, and you can see a short slide-presentation (in Dutch and English) explaining the background and origins of the house. Note also the charming garden in formal style, unusually large

for Amsterdam.
*Open*: Daily 11.00 to 17.00
*Closed*: 1 January

### ◆
### ZOOLOGISCH MUSEUM
*Plantage Middenlaan 53*
Exhibitions about animal life, their evolution, etc. Attached to the Artis Zoo. This is perhaps a rather specialist museum, interesting, but the main reason for its existence is as an extension of the Zoo's research.
*Open*: Daily 09.00 to 17.00

### Other Places of Interest
The great array of 17th-century buildings is the main attraction of Amsterdam today, principally in the brick and gabled buildings seen on every side. Amongst them, however, are other unusual buildings and sites, some being unique in Europe – the impressive Dam Square on the site of the first settlement raised above the water, the spectacular gilded and coronetted churches rising with stately steeples to make exclamation marks above the red roof-tops, the canals themselves with drooping trees along which the rich merchants built some very expensive and gorgeously furnished houses some of which can be visited to give an idea of life in such families 300 years ago, the wide waters of the port beyond the Centraal Station, the human associations that reach out and touch a nerve in our own day such as the justly famous house of Anne Frank where the attic hid the family and still tells a tale

*The Willet-Holthuysen Museum, authentically furnished and a perfect example of a 17th-century patrician canal house*

and, yes, the Red Light District which is often the reason some tourists come to Amsterdam and which still thrives as a centre for the oldest profession the world knows.

◆◆
## AALSMEER
A fascinating visit can be made to the flower auctions that are held in this suburb. You will need to go early to see the loads of flowers arriving on special carts which are taken into auction rooms and sold at great speed using a timing system – large clocks are connected to a computer system which keeps track of sales (you will be baffled to understand how the place works, the pace is so fast). The centre is huge yet well organised for visitors – you pay a small entrance fee and then are conducted along walkways over the auction floors, looking down on massed blooms on the floors beneath.

To visit the flower auction you will need to take a bus to the World Flower Centre. For details and times of opening, which can vary, check at VVV Tourist offices which can also give you the date of the flower parade (the Bloemencorso) which is usually the first Saturday of September and follows a route from the auction centre to Amsterdam and back. The auctions, the biggest in the world and seemingly a sea of blooms, are over by 09.30.

◆◆
## BEGIJNHOF
*The Spui*
Ancient settlement of religious foundation with old houses around courts, giving a strong impression of old Amsterdam life. Here you are in a silent part of the city, and can appreciate how this little community lived. Notable are several of the houses, original buildings in styles of their period. Not to be missed.

◆◆◆
## DAM SQUARE (THE DAM)
The heart of the city and always crowded, Dam Square is the place to wander around and get the 'feel' of things – from the shoppers crowding towards the walking areas of the main shopping streets to the layabouts. Everything you need from post office to department store is a few steps from the Dam.

*Flower stalls are an essential part of the Amsterdam scene; this one is part of Singel Flower Market*

◆◆
### FLOWER MARKET
Along the Singel, open stalls and boats, a mass of flowers at all seasons.

◆
### HOLLANDSE SCHOUWBURG
*Off Plantage Kerklaan*
Now a shell, but a national monument because of its importance in World War II – here the Jews of Amsterdam were herded together before deportation in a building that had played host to Jewish entertainers performing for the local audience. There is a simple yet impressive monument and the site is a park, still stark with memories.

◆◆◆
### KONINKLIJK PALACE
*The Dam*
A must for every visitor to Amsterdam. Although no one lives here now it is an imposing and grandiose pile of masonry and you cannot miss it in its central position at the end of the Dam Square. It is a palace in name only, having started life as an administrative building, and later being made into a palatial residence by Napoleon Buonaparte for his brother who was declared King of the Netherlands. The next monarch after Napoleon's downfall also occupied the place, and so it continued for a century until the city administration acquired it and restored it in 1935. The interior is fascinating yet stern and heavy, with many marble sculptures and bas-reliefs, as well as vast painted ceilings and much gilded plasterwork.

Don't miss the Marble Tribunal, the huge relief map of the city in early times, or the Civic Hall, which is on the first floor.
The façade of the palace is plain and severe.
*Open*: daily in summer 12.30 to 16.00. Guided tours every Wednesday.

◆◆
### LEIDSEPLEIN
One of the attractions of Amsterdam is the varied street life, and you will usually find a great deal to see and listen to just strolling along the streets of Leidseplein. Here the crowds range around listening to individual musicians, groups, mimes, singers and comedians, all using the street as their pitch and of course hoping for the occasional handout. Some of the talent on offer can be surprisingly good, and almost all are young and hopeful just needing an audience to express their talents and get a round of applause. The crowds are good-natured and a rapport often builds up between performers and public that makes this casual street entertainment even more appealing.

◆
### LUTHERSE KERK
*Singel, corner of Kattengat*
No longer a church (part of a hotel), the massive green dome is a central city landmark.

◆◆
### MONTELBAANSTOREN
*Beside the Oude Schans waterway*

## WHAT TO SEE – OTHER PLACES OF INTEREST

A handsome tower, a landmark with its striking double cupola, this is a part of the old defensive system of walls and towers that once protected Amsterdam. It stands in the middle of an old nautical area, and now holds offices that control the water levels in the city's canals.

*The Montelbaanstoren, on the Oude Schans canal. The tower was part of the 15th-century defences*

◆
### MOZES EN AARONKERK
*Waterlooplein*
This large and imposing church dates in its present state from the 19th century. It stands in the swirl of the Flea Market and is now a centre for

help and a place for locals to meet. Its cavernous interior, beneath the twin towers, houses exhibitions and is a crowded, popular and lively place.

◆◆
### MUNTPLEIN
*City centre*
The Munt means mint, and one operated here in the early 17th century when the French invaded the Netherlands and the country's mint had to be moved to a safe place: it was

transferred here to this little tower, the *Munttoren*, which formed part of the city's fortifications. This fine round tower, illuminated in summer, makes an exclamation mark and can be seen as you walk down the Rokin from the Dam Square. The river once ran here. It was moved and the square is now one of the busiest in Amsterdam with lots of traffic and trams. On the island occupied by the Munttoren are tourist aids and it is also a meeting point for friends.

◆
## NATIONAL MONUMENT
*Dam Square*

A rather uninspired design, like a spacecraft emerging from a silo under the square, a stone obelisk surmounts a platform on which are grouped several figures representing peace, resistance and the tragedies of war. It is a pity that it is artistically so commonplace for it means a lot to the Dutch, commemorating as it does the many victims of war. It has become a central meeting point. Each year in May a ceremony is held here honouring the war dead – at 20.00 on 8 May there is a two-minute silence, nationally observed.

◆◆
## NIEUWE KERK
*The Dam*

New church really means newer than the old one, and this Gothic church is an important centre and coronation church. With its fine, high-arched interior, it reminds you of Dutch paintings of churches in the Golden Age. There is much to see, from intricate carving to the great organ. It is no longer a 'working' church, having no parish, but is used for concerts, exhibitions and state functions. Construction started in the 15th century, but took many years – foundations in the city are always a problem, and many of the houses are based on logs driven deep into the North Sea mud below (so it is not surprising that in Amsterdam some of the tallest buildings are still the church towers). The Nieuwe Kerk was the setting for the coronation of Queen Beatrix in 1980.
*Open*: Monday to Saturday 11.00 to 16.00; Sundays 12.00 to 17.00
*Closed*: January, February
Small admission charge.

◆
## NIEUWE MARKT AND WAAG

An open space in the east of the city where the Waag, or Weigh House, stands. You can pause and sit here, beside the canal, to enjoy the quiet scene. The Waag looks like a medieval castle with its pointed towers among the trees – this is appropriate because it dates from 1488. The square was the setting for demonstrations when the nearby Metro station was being constructed – many old houses were threatened, an old working-class neighbourhood was disrupted, and the Dutch believe in giving voice when they think important things are at stake.

Although markets can be found all over the city (see Shopping, page 77) there is no longer one here, although on Sundays from spring to September the Nieuwe Markt is the setting for an antiques fair.

◆
**NOORDERKERK**
*off Westerstraat, the Jordaan*
This big construction of brick in the form of a Greek cross is still a working Protestant church. If it is open do go inside – it is unusual and impressive. Built in 1622, it is a stern, formal building, yet the pews and chairs, now grouped in the middle, give it a comfortable local air. See the vast sounding board over the pulpit, and if you can attend a Saturday morning concert (very impromptu, from 10.00 to 12.00) then you will probably get a free cup of coffee too!

◆
**NORMAAL AMSTERDAMS PEIL**
*City Hall/Muziektheater, Waterlooplein (basement)*
The water levels of this historic town are of great import. This fascinating geological exhibition shows, among other things, the difference in levels in the North Sea, the Ijsselmeer and Amsterdam.

◆◆
**OLD JEWISH QUARTER**
This is a must for anyone with Jewish connections, but it is also a fascinating part of old Amsterdam, even if many of the original buildings are now gone. It stretches east of the city, its main thoroughfare being the Jodenbreestraat, now almost all modern. Synagogues and statues show Jewish historical points and the Hollandse Schouwburg is a monument. Now a ruin, it was the centre of World War II deportations.

◆◆
**OUDE KERK**
*Ouderkerksplein 23*
The 'Old Church' stands in a small cobbled square, encircled by charming houses – but it is also in the middle of the Red Light District. It is worth a long visit for its recently restored paintings and impressive, beamed interior. The tower, a delicate and unusual construction with much detail and colour, can be climbed at certain times Monday to Thursday in summer months.
*Open*: Monday to Saturday 11.00 to 16.00; winter 13.00 to 15.00
*Closed*: Sunday, festive days.

◆
**PORTUGUESE SYNAGOGUE**
*Visserplein*
An imposing building that managed to escape destruction at the hands of the Nazis in World War II. It dates from the 17th century when the Jewish population was increasing in the city, and by its very size and sumptuous interior indicates the power of the new immigrants. (Jews were given much more opportunity to settle and expand in the Netherlands than elsewhere in Europe, and in Amsterdam they became an

*Nieuwe Kerk, on Dam Square, coronation church of Dutch monarchs since 1814*

important part of city life with banking and insurance interests to the fore in a society fast becoming affluent. Jews were allowed self-government, and in the late 18th century were given civic status.) The synagogue was restored in the 1950s. (Discreet dress and head-covering required.)

◆◆
## RAILWAY STATION
(*Stationsplein*)
An imposing, grandiose 19th-century monumental building in the approved palatial style, the Centraal Station was 100 years old in 1989, having been built by the same architect who designed the Rijksmuseum. Ornate, even flamboyant, the themes of its external decoration glorify travel and the sea.

## WHAT TO SEE – OTHER PLACES OF INTEREST

### ◆◆◆
### THE RED LIGHT DISTRICT

The liberal attitude of the Amsterdam native towards things sexual is sometimes surprising to the visitor, yet inevitably the tourists flock in to the famous Red Light District to view the goings-on. It is a fairly compact area east of the Dam Square in the maze of little alleys and streets along the old canals of the OZ Voorburgwal and the OZ Achterburgwal and around the great rearing tower of the Oude Kerk. Here you will see, seated demurely in pink-lit windows, the famed 'girls' of Amsterdam, sometimes displaying obvious attractions and always clad in the scantiest little bits of lace and satin, occasionally with a side-prop such as a whip or some fetishist object to indicate their 'specialities'. The house may be marked with a red light, or the premises may be little more than a shop window and the 'display areas' are certainly not home – most of the women come in from the suburbs to work a regular shift of eight hours, changing duty, it is said, three times a day so the action is a round-the-clock one. There is a range of women to be looked at – from the exotic Indonesian to the homely round-faced local, from the teenager to the nearly gone-to-seed – it is indeed, a

*. . . Amsterdam's Red Light District is world-famous*

profession where the more experience you have the less money you can expect to get. A lot of people are literally 'window shopping', just walking around and looking at the sights, but men on their own or in male-only groups can expect to get winked at and gesticulated at. When someone nets a customer the curtains are closed very rapidly or in some alleys a door is locked, and for a few minutes it is play-time for the hooked fish, work-time for the woman. Amsterdam has had the Red Light District for many centuries, probably as long as it has been a port, and it is controlled by the city with regular check-ups for disease and a register. The women themselves can be quite militant and in this city of toleration and mutual concern even a prostitute has her rights as a citizen. The women have their own organisations and have grouped to pressure the council for a fair deal.

The Red Light District is fairly contained within the central area specified, but in recent years it has also extended towards the Singel and even into one or two of the streets crossing the outer canals, and in the alleys off the Nieuwendijk you will come across sex shops and tattoo parlours, as well as sex cinemas. Sex is quite a business in Amsterdam, and it certainly encourages tourism. Beside the pink-lit windows you will find the ubiquitous sex shops, peddling magazines, pictures, videos for even the most arcane tastes. Do not look if you are likely to be offended, for photographs and sex-aids, some of them quite bizarre, are on full view in the brightly lit windows.

There are many peep-shows and sex-exhibitions too, and you can wander through them to have a look, even if you don't want to pop a guilder, or a five guilder piece, into a machine in a booth. Again, all tastes seem to be catered for, so don't enter if you are likely to dislike what you see. A complaint even to a police officer would only result in a shrug and probably an unbelieving smile. Few people go into the Red Light District without being fully aware of what's on offer there. When walking in this part of town keep to the main streets, especially at night, and make sure your wallet or purse is safe – naturally enough this part of town attracts all sorts of characters and at street corners you cannot help but notice the drug addicts. Gangs of two or three can easily corner an unwary tourist who has gone into a quiet or dead-end street, and it happens often enough for you to take proper precautions. It is a pity to have to keep repeating the warning, but do take care and exercise obvious precautions when strolling in the city.

This part of Amsterdam is a magnet for gay men, and information on the city can be obtained from a 24-hour telephone service at (20) 23 63 65 (also information for women). There are gay cinemas as well as heterosexual ones, and a free paper in English, *The Gay Amsterdam News*, is available in bars and clubs. Several hotels in the city also offer accommodation to men only. Mixed in with the lurid cinemas and sex-shops are very ordinary and welcoming pubs and cafés, and people live their lives in the flats and houses right in the district. The situation, which may seem an extraordinary paradox to people not used to such straightforwardness, is underlined in the little cobbled square around the impressive Oude Kerk – for here religion faces the oldest profession, and there are even pink windows right up against the church. Lust and devotion exist side by side and seem to manage very well too, but then that is just a part of the unique atmosphere of this surprising city.

◆
### SCHREIERSTOREN
*Zeedijk*
This tower was part of the city defences and the name means 'tower of tears'. From here wives and sweethearts waved goodbye to departing sailors from the city walls as their ships faded from sight.

◆◆
### SINT ANDRIESHOFJE
*The Jordaan, 107 Egalantiersgracht*
You will need to look hard for the small door that admits you to these almshouses – a *hofje* means a small house. Grouped around the tranquil garden, the

*Magere Brug, or 'Skinny Bridge'*

houses have black doors with names on them, and neat tiled roofs.

◆
### SINT NICOLAAS KERK
*Prins Hendrikkade*
This is the major Roman Catholic church in the city and is associated with a miracle that supposedly occurred in the Middle Ages off the city's

central Kalverstraat. A shrine was built on the Heligeweg, called the Chapel of the Host, to commemorate the event (a dying man, being offered the host by a priest, could not take it and it was thrown into a fire but refused to burn). The chapel burned in the 15th century and St Nicolaas has taken over the annual celebration. At the time of the November Christmas parade, the church is the finishing point of the procession.

◆◆
## SKINNY BRIDGE (MAGERE BRUG)

The best known bridge on the wide Amstel is the so-called Skinny Bridge, a drawbridge running into Kerkstraat. Once there were many such bridges in the city. Now this is a much-loved landmark.

◆
**TRIPPENHUIS**
*Kloveniersburgwal 29*
Although this grandly imposing manor house on a canal is no longer a museum it did once house the national collection, later to be the Rijksmuseum, in the last century. The house itself, once owned by the fabulously rich Tripp brothers who made their fortune from iron and armaments (note the oddly shaped chimneys) is a 17th-century classical façade, all pilasters and ornamental swags.

◆
**UNIVERSITY AREA**
The University buildings are to be found around the Spui and the Singel and the area is a gathering place for the young.

*Clogs are still worn in country areas but most are now made for tourists and for townspeople to use as decorative plantholders*

◆
**VOORBURGWAL**
Together with the Achterburgwal this forms the central part of the city – straight canals where the original port was laid out. These old canal streets are still very beautiful despite being part of the Red Light District, and there are many fine brick houses interspersed with well-designed modern houses here and there which do not break the house-line.

◆
**WESTERKERK**
*Westermarkt*
The crown-topped spire which

rises above the small cobbled square by the canal is a city landmark – for decades it was the tallest building in the city. It is still a working church and can be visited. It dates from the early years of the 17th century and Rembrandt is supposedly buried here though no one knows where. There is a memorial to the painter near the grave of his son, Titus. The gleaming red and yellow crown lifted high over the neighbouring houses is a supposed replica of the one presented to the city by the Emperor Maximilian in 1489. Concerts take place here, often using the fine organ. Outside there is a statue of Anne Frank who lived near by.

♦♦
## ZOO AND AQUARIUM
*Kerklaan 40*
The Artis Zoo is an extensive zoological garden and aquarium located in the southeastern section of the city. Here you can see all sorts of animals, in areas as nearly approximating to their original habitats as possible, and many kinds of birds. The zoo is not large, yet the lay-out gives a sense of spaciousness, and there are many interesting plants and trees – every year in March there is a major flower show in the grounds (*Artis Staat in Bloei*). There is also a very large and comprehensive aquarium and a planetarium which uses a large screen projector for probing looks at the stars. Beside the zoo (on Plantage

Middenlaan 53) is the Zoologisch Museum with special changing shows of animal life, their evolution and habits. Zoo entry includes ticket for the museum, otherwise a separate fee is made at the Plantage Middenlaan entry.
The zoo itself, which for long was a private membership organisation, and only opened to the general public in 1937, was 150 years old in 1988. There is a little farmyard incorporated in the zoo, especially for children, where domestic animals can be seen and tended; there is usually a number of young animals here, too.
On Plantage Parklaan not far from the zoo are the University's Botanical Gardens, with many unusual plants and trees, as well as greenhouses for tropical and exotic items. Small admission charge, café.
*Open:* all year: 09.00 to 18.00, earlier closing in winter months.

♦
## ZUIDERKERK
*Off the Sint Antoniesbreestraat*
Enter the quiet courtyard of this imposing church from a gateway surmounted by skulls and crossbones, gilded bones decorating a 17th-century arch. The church is surrounded by a modern development, a well-designed enclave where the only sound is of children playing. The church itself is a handsome one – early 17th-century and with a gilded spire, part painted in maroon. No longer used for worship the

church itself is now a community centre. You can climb the tower. Nice views of quiet canals in the pleasant neighbourhood.
*Open*: 1 June to 15 October: Wednesday 14.00 – 17.00, Thursday and Friday 11.00 – 14.00, Saturday until 16.00. Allow 45 minutes.

### Walks
### A Walk along the Canals
You could take any one of the three major 'later canals' constructed in the 17th century (the Herengracht, the Keizersgracht and the Prinsengracht) and see a good deal, and it is easy to swing from one to another given their lay-out and planning. Any walk in Amsterdam is very flexible and this one particularly so but since the **Herengracht** is undoubtedly the grandest canal and possesses the most impressive houses start with this one, up at its juncture with the harbour, a short walk from the station. Immediately you leave the busy central station area and start your walk along the waterway you will notice the calm and peace. You could, however, start your stroll a little further back at the Harbour Building (the **Havengebouw**) overlooking the waters of the Ij and the modern port of Amsterdam, marked with many developments. There is a restaurant at the top of this building and not far away, if you want to see more of the harbour, is the free ferry (near the Centraal Station) called the Buiksloterweg Ferry. You will

get a better idea of the working of the harbour than from the regular hire boats that cross Het Ij. Walk back into the town from the Prins Hendrikkade and across the Haarlemmerstraat find the entrance to the Herengracht. This is the smartest of the 'grachts' and in the late 17th century this 'gentlemen's canal' was *the* place to live, especially further down towards the Amstel.
Along these canals you will see a procession of gables of all kinds – the official appellations are 'neck', 'spout' or 'clock', and you should be able to spot all three versions quickly enough. Some of the houses date back to the early

years of the blossoming 17th century and while many were the mansions of rich merchants, others have resounding associations – Peter the Great, on his extensive and supposedly anonymous tour of Europe, lived on the Herengracht while in Amsterdam.

Along the parallel Keizersgracht ('Emperors' Canal') you will find a parade of stepped gables, and, at numbers 12 and 16, a fantasy of plumes and urns. Note the fanlights over the entrance doors, such as 111 with

*An interesting study can be made of the magnificently decorative canal house gables*

garlands. At 123 a redbrick palace offers a striking façade of the early 17th century (1622), a local monument with busts of classical heroes crowned with grapes, feathers and helmets, the whole swagged with garlands and suggesting well the affluence of new money of the time. The gables continue along the canal in a welter of whipped cream, the plaster in general is well kept up and the buildings are clean. Note that many of them are not actually joined together, and although they all seem to hold each other up at times, you can often see a slice of space between the houses. Later houses have cupids and typical 18th-century motifs. Sometimes you will get a look down a corridor inside one of the houses and a glimpse of an ornate interior, often cluttered with the inevitable parked bicycles! Occasionally you will see an unpainted house, such as at 387 with fruits, garlands, flowers and swags in a soft natural stone.

The little lanes that connect the three canals (the exterior one is the Prinsengracht) are often almost countrylike in their appeal – the Molenpad, for example, has trees and creepers hanging from houses (off the Keizersgracht and near the Leidsegracht).

A series of canals cut across the main ones, and you might like to turn and explore the Leidsegracht, a pretty canal paralleling the busy Leidsestraat near by. The noise assails you as you approach this busy street, so

# GREATER AMSTERDAM

0    500   1000   1500   2000 metres

S102

N5

BOS EN LOMMER

GEUZENVELD

Erasmus
Park

SLOTERMEER

OUD WEST

Sloter
Park

OVERTOOMSE
VELD

Sloterplas

Rembrandt
Park

OSDORP

Vondel
Park

Van Gogh
Museum

SLOTERVAART

NIEUWE

SLOTEN

Olympic
Stadium

Beatrix
Park

A4

A10

Het Nieuwe Meer

NIEUWE
MEER

Bosbaan

BUITENVELDERT

Grote
Vijver

Amsterdamse Bos

AMSTELVEEN

Luchthaven
Schiphol

## WHAT TO SEE – WALKS

continue to detour along the Leidsegracht. A new policy of keeping the road as narrow as possible on these back canals seems to be in force – some of them have very high, yellow-painted kerbs just wide enough for two regular sized vehicles to pass, and they can hardly go fast along such narrow traffic lanes.

Continue to the Prinsengracht and walk on the left along the Vijzelstraat. Where it crosses the Keizersgracht look for number 672, the **Van Loon Museum**, noted as the house of the artist Ferdinand Bol. This is another canal house kept as it once was and, in addition to the family antiques (the Van Loons lived here for many years), there is a series of portraits (open Mondays only). On the other side of this same canal is the **Fodor Museum** at Keizersgracht 609 (see page 27), a collection constantly changing of the work of Dutch artists. It is an offshoot of the Stedelijk and has special shows in summer, mostly of Amsterdam artists. Return along the Vijzelstraat to the Herengracht and turn right. This part of the canal is replete with large mansions with imposing doors and armorial bearings. The mayor of the city has an official residence at 502, and the Czar's house was 527. You can glimpse something of the social life of the time, however, at the **Willet-Holthuysen** house at Herengracht 605. This is real Dutch grandeur of the time, and the big doubled-fronted house is filled with the most

opulent treasures. You cannot miss the beflagged front and the palatial aspect of this canal house, and if you see only one interior, then this really has to be it (see page 32). Outside is a rare example of a period garden, running over to the Amstelstraat where it is screened by a railed grille from the busy street.

Continue along the Herengracht to its junction with the Amstel (an exotic gable at 568–570 has writhing bird-headed beasts) passing a new development – number 610, a house which now has reflecting mirror in its old window frames. Fine views across the Amstel with the bridges on the opposite shore well lined up for a photograph, and up the river as far as the old Amstel Hotel. Turn along the Amstel with the **Blauwbrug** (no longer blue, but a stone structure that apes one in Paris) to your right. A diamond factory is on the corner at number 209 Amstel. Go along Amstelstraat to see the garden of the Willet-Holthuysen Museum, cross in to the pedestrian street opposite and take in the view of the new Muziektheater across the water. A short walk along the Amstel will take you to the Muntplein with small shops along the landside – antiques at number 208, a tiny shop with some good glass – and the Holthuysen-Stoeltie diamond factory on the Wagennstraat. As an alternative walk to the right along the Amstel from its junction with the Herengracht and look for the **Six Collection** at 218 Amstel (the Six Collectie). Here you can find the Rembrandt portrait of Jan Six, along with other Rembrandts and 17th-century masterworks. A small, very choice collection and you will need an invitation which can be obtained by applying to the Rijksmuseum. Opposite, the Amstel is bridged with its most famous drawbridge, running into the Kerkstraat. This is the **Skinny Bridge** (Magere Brug) a relic of the wooden bridges that once were common throughout Amsterdam and a landmark much loved by Amsterdammers. Walk back along the Kerkstraat, turning right at the Reguliersgracht and go up to the

*The bright lights of bars, nightclubs and cafés in Rembrandtsplein*

**Rembrandtsplein** where there are many cafés surrounding a garden with a sculpture of the painter. This is a major centre for nightlife. Opposite is an arcade under a bank building with showcases of modern art. Walk back to the Muntplein along Reguliersbreestraat to find a mixture of shops including Kwekkeboom which sells good pastries and chocolates and a marvellous 1920s cinema which is a monument of its time – the **Tuschinski Theatre**, named after its creator and an exotic specimen of the period of Art Deco both inside and out.

**A Walk around The Jordaan**
This makes a pleasant short exploration of a charming and relatively unvisited quarter of Amsterdam without any major

## WHAT TO SEE – WALKS

tourist sights save the church beside the Herengracht, the Westerkerk. A well-defined area of narrow slanted streets on the northwest side of the city, it is filled with pleasing little houses and shops both old and new, and has a neighbourly atmosphere and a 'feel' of being a separate town even though it is located conveniently between the Herengracht and the Lijnbaansgracht beyond the city entry road, the Rozengracht.

The area is small and notable for the fact that all its streets seem to slant in an almost wilful pattern away from the main 'grachts'. This is explained by the fact that prior to 1600 this was open fields with drainage canals running diagonally to the city walls, and the plan has remained unaltered. (The name is a corruption of the French word 'jardin' or garden.) For centuries it was a working-class district and only in the past 40 years after a complete furbishment in the late 1940s has it been a neighbourhood considered worth living in.

Start the walk from the Westermarkt, at the **Westerkerk** with its crown-topped spire. A graceful landmark, for a long time this elegant tower was the tallest building in the city. It is still a working church, dating from the early years of the 17th century, and Rembrandt is reputed to be buried here – there is a memorial near the grave of his son, Titus. The gleaming yellow and red crown lifted high over the local canals is a supposed replica of the one presented to the city by Emperor Maximilian in 1489. Concerts can be heard inside (there is a fine organ) and the interior is worth a visit for its high, spare simplicity. Outside there is a statue of Anne Frank (the house and museum is near by at Prinsengracht 263). In summer the **Anne Frankhuis** can become a very popular spot with long lines of people waiting to get in.

Walk down the Rozengracht until you reach Erste Bloemdwarstraat, making little humps as it crosses the Jordaan canals. The neat redbrick houses cluster closely, there are unusual stone plaques set in the walls, small shops, creepers growing over old façades. Modern buildings have been well integrated, sometimes complete with jokes as with the large water tap sticking out on the Tuinstraat. At the Egelantiersgracht turn right and walk along the canal to number 107 where a door (the central one) opens to admit you to a tiny garden and a set of early 17th-century almshouses that seem out of this world. This is the Sint Andrieshofje (a *hofje* is a small house), once a very necessary social need in an impoverished community. The almshouses have black doors with names on them, and old tile roofs. The Bloemgracht was the better place to live once upon a time, but now the parallel Egelantiersgracht is just as charming – there are ducks and the herons are almost tame as they sit hunched on the banks. Follow it to the Prinsengracht and note the café on the corner – Café Smalle, famous for being the original place where Genever gin was first distilled. Across

*The steeple of the Westerkerk, topped by a shining crown and orb*

the street is a parade of houses along the Prinsengracht, a variety of styles, often large-shuttered, one with a fake classical front of jokey urns and a balustrade, and extraordinary windows. Cross the leafy Westerstraat and enter the small square by the **Noorderkerk**, a looming construction that is still a working Protestant church. It is

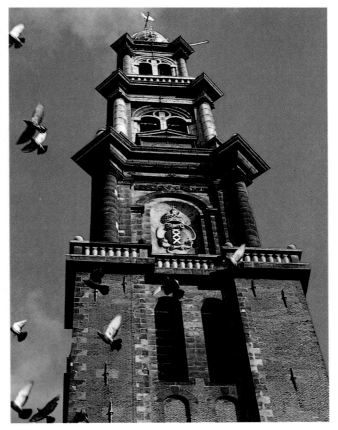

worth going in if you can because its design is unusual. Built in 1622, it is a stern, formal building in the unusual shape of a Greek X, yet the pews and chairs in the centre give it a comfortable air. Over the pulpit is an enormous sounding board. Go on a Saturday morning for an organ concert, very impromptu, from 10.00 to 12.00, and quite probably a free cup of coffee too! Around the church on Saturday a market unfolds, with a few stalls selling cage-birds. The market extends down the nearby street, very busy on a Saturday morning, very local in flavour. Retrace your steps, or cross to a parallel street to take you up to the Brouwersgracht (try the Lindengracht). Look for a famous 'brown bar' at this point, Papeneiland, old and atmospheric. In the distance, in the central city, rises the one-time **Lutheran Church**, its massy green dome still a landmark.

A short walk along the Harlemmerstraat (or the slightly more northerly Harlemmerdijk) will take you through a busy, crowded neighbourhood with many small shops and cafés and a pleasing, friendly atmosphere towards the centre of town and

*Stretcher bearers displaying the round yellow local cheeses at Alkmaar cheesemarket*

the Stationsplein. Visit the Jordaan by day or night, but Saturdays and Sundays when there are things going on are best bets, and local people are out walking and shopping with the children in tow.

**Excursions from Amsterdam**

In Holland nothing is very far from anywhere else and in this small, compact country with its excellent transport system and roads you can go to numerous places of interest for a day or half-a-day's excursion. A trip into typical countryside is easy, if only to see windmills with whirring arms, or the blaze of coloured stripes that the fields become in bulb-flowering time. Coach outings are organised at bulb blossom time (ask the VVV Amsterdam Tourist Office or your local Dutch tourist office for details), or marked routes assist the independent driver or cyclist. Practically all of Holland's towns are well served by rail, or if you wish to take a guided tour then there are many operating by bus from Amsterdam's Stationsplein or from the Dam, but these will rarely allow time for visits to museums, although good for those with limited time.

◆

**ALKMAAR, EDAM, GOUDA**

A group of cheese-producing towns which have picturesque markets where the round yellow and red cheeses are piled neatly onto stretchers (check market dates with the VVV). Market days are highly photogenic, and the towns are also old and atmospheric with many brick buildings, mullioned windows and gables. At Alkmaar the cheeses are weighed on large machines, and attendants are often dressed in national costume with women in lace and black dresses and men wearing the typical clogs. Also at Alkmaar, which is the most attractive and therefore most crowded of the cheese-producing towns, there is a cheese museum. You will usually be able to view old cheese-making and weighing equipment, and on *non* market days these old settlements make charming walks with few tourists.

◆◆

**DELFT**

A very typical Dutch town with a crowded and attractive market and fine brick houses and churches. It is a busy place with many shops and things to see, so plan a day and have lunch here – you can buy wonderful snacks at market stalls, from the ever popular smoked fish to hot sandwiches and pickles. Delft is a walking town of course, with lots of narrow, tree-shaded canals and many opportunities for photographs. There are brick pavements, narrow humped bridges and barges and boats. The churches have the big towers one associates with Dutch churches and the **Nieuwe Kerk** here has an added prominence – it is the burial place for members of the Dutch royal family. A fee is charged to go round the

## WHAT TO SEE – EXCURSIONS

church, also to climb the tower for views across the neighbouring countryside. The other major church is the **Oude Kerk** and it has a tower with a decided lean! This church was begun in 1250 and within is a parade of monuments (note the famed Maarten Tromp monument, a battle at sea, all sculpted in marble, also the curiously carved pulpit). Near here is the **Prinsenhof**, a mansion which started life as a convent. Now it is a museum of the municipality. The scene of the shooting of William the Silent, it is open every day. At each end of the central **markt** are imposing buildings, one the Nieuwe Kerk already mentioned and the other the **Stadhuis**, or town hall, while the VVV Amsterdam Tourist Office is between the two. The famous product is, of course, the pottery and you will find it everywhere from

*Distinctive Delftware: a demonstration of handpainting at a Delft porcelain factory*

market stalls to tourist shops. Watch out for cheap reproductions if you want a good piece, and it is a wise idea to visit the **Lambert van Meerten Museum** at 119 Oude Delft (open every day, admission fee). Here you will find an enormous showing of Delft ware from tea cups to tiles. It is a good introduction to the ware, which when genuine is marked with an imprint. One of the porcelain factories can be visited at 196 Rotterdamseweg.

The famous son of Delft is the painter Vermeer – a remarkable and mysterious master of the 17th century whose work is only to be found in major museums such as those in Washington and New York or in London's National

Gallery. There are examples in the Amsterdam Rijksmuseum, and a large canvas in The Hague is an actual View of Delft.

◆◆
### HAARLEM

A large town and only a short journey across the flat fields of the westernmost part of Holland to this capital of a province. The town has a spacious and calm central **Grote Markt** surrounded with elegant Renaissance buildings and the great looming shape of the church of **St Bavo**. It is well worth a visit, being a typical large Dutch church with numerous chapels and a famous organ which has been played by Mozart, Handel and other composers.

The painter Frans Hals, best known of Haarlem's sons, is buried here and his works form a magnificent legacy to a town that did not treat him well – he passed his old age in great poverty. The pictures can be seen in a museum dedicated to him, the **Frans Hals Museum**, housed in a one-time hospice for aged men. His works are stars in foreign collections – his *Laughing Cavalier*, familiar from reproductions, hangs in the Wallace Collection in London. The museum surrounds a charming 17th-century courtyard and there are also works by other artists, with a special wing for modern art. (Open every day except Mondays, from 13.00 on Sundays and holidays).

Also in Haarlem is the oldest museum in Holland, the **Teylers Collection**, housed in an impressive set of rooms. Here you will find scientific exhibits reflecting the age in which they were collected and made, and the objects cover a diverse range from gemstones to scientific models, equipment and instruments. The overall feeling is indeed of an historic place, for the display cases are all in traditional style. (Open every day except Mondays; Sundays from 13.00.)

A new place in Haarlem is the house which parallels Anne Frank's attic in Amsterdam, for here, at Barteljorisstraat 19, you will find a place where many Jewish refugees hid during the war. Recently opened, this monument may not have quite the tragic aspects of Anne's story, but it reveals the bravery of Mrs Corrie ten Boom who hid desperate people here and later wrote about it in a book, *The Hiding Place*. It is a house to touch the heart.

A day should be allocated to Haarlem, for there is much to see in this canal-bordered city. The **Stadhuis** (town hall) is open every weekday and has origins going back to the medieval era. Near by, on the market square, the **Meat Hall** and the **Fish Hall**, were once covered markets, now galleries of the museum.

◆
### HEEMSTEDE

An interesting little town with many fine houses, an early 17th-century church and the remains of a medieval castle.

# CENTRAL AMSTERDAM

This was where the Swedish botanist Linnaeus lived from 1735 while working on the collections of an Amsterdam plant enthusiast. There is a museum showing a restored steam pump operation.

◆
## HOORN
In the north of the country (the town which gave its name to Cape Horn), this place has a beguiling country-town charm.

## KEUKENHOF GARDENS
See Lisse, below.

◆
## LEIDEN
This is the seat of Holland's most ancient university, and the town is handsome and not only possesses museums but also has associations with the Pilgrim Fathers on their peregrinations around Europe in search of tolerance for their beliefs. There is a **Pilgrim Fathers Centre** at 45 Vliet (open Monday to Friday), and John Robinson, one of the guiding lights of the group, is buried at the vast brick **Church of St Peter** in the centre of the town.
The centre of Leiden is handsome and well preserved. For 400 years the university's buildings have been along the Rapenburg with the **Academie**, reflected in the canal, the main centre. The VVV Tourist Office is on the Stationsplein, and you can take boat rides on the waterways. The museums include the **Rijksmuseum** (National Museum of Antiquities) at 28 Rapenburg (open every day

except Mondays) and the **Lakenhal**, which is now the municipal museum but was once the guildhall of the clothmakers (open every day except Mondays). Here you will find paintings (Rembrandt was from Leiden) and local crafts. The Army Museum (**Legermuseum**) at 7 Pesthuisiaan is a collection of weapons and memorabilia and the **Rijksmuseum Voor Volkenkunde**, 1 Steenstraat, covers the subject of ethnology (open every day except Mondays).

◆◆
## LISSE
In this town near Haarlem you will find the famous **Keukenhof Gardens**. Here, in spring, there is a parade of blossom, and the setting is ravishing with wooded dells and grassy spaces. This is in the middle of the tulip area and so is very popular for tourists in spring but the gardens maintain their charm all year round. Near by are extensive sand dunes.

◆
## MIDDELBURG
A good distance from Amsterdam, but if you wish to see people in national costume worn as an everyday dress, it is one of the places to visit. Here you will find a small, redbrick town in the middle of the wide flat marshland of the south and on market days Middelburg attracts in local people.

◆
## ROTTERDAM
A modern city, almost totally

destroyed in the last war, Rotterdam has risen again in a striking modern design and is now the centre of the world's busiest seaport, **Europoort**. It has much to offer, even if all its ancient houses and most of its historical associations are now memories. There is a gallery of major importance, the **Boymans-Van Beuningen Museum** (Flemish and Dutch masters and a modern collection make this a place to note. Open every day except Mondays.)

*Tulips near Amsterdam – literally millions of them, at the Keukenhof Gardens in Lisse*

A part of the town that has been preserved in its ancient style is **Delftshaven**, the quarter from which the Pilgrim Fathers departed in 1620. The birthplace of Erasmus, Rotterdam offers city and port tours. Check at the VVV Tourist Office either at the **Centraal Station**, or by the **Stadhuis**.

◆◆
THE HAGUE
Plan a whole day here: there is lots to see and do. It is the centre of government and is close to the sea with a beach at **Scheveningen**. The main attraction here is the

**Binnenhof**, a part of the castle of the Counts of Holland standing on the Hof Vijver ornamental lake. It is now the home of the Dutch government and the two chambers meet in the 13th-century **Ridderzaal** which can be visited, when not in use, on a conducted tour. The hall is the setting of the state opening of Parliament by the monarch.

William V's collection can be seen at the **Schilderijenzaal Prins Willem V** (open daily from 11.00) and is a typical 18th-century picture collection. It stands in the **Buitenhof**, the old outer court of the original castle. Near by is the old **Prison Gate** with a collection of torture instruments (Gevangenpoort), open every day from May to September). In the Binnenhof court is a small museum that should not be missed on any account – the **Mauritshuis** has a very fine collection of paintings of Holland's great age; this Royal Picture Gallery is housed in a renovated Renaissance palace. Also in The Hague is the **Oude Stadhuis** of the 16th century, the **Grote Kerk**, several other notable museums and a curiosity, the **Panorama Mesdeg** with a huge circular painting of 19th-century Scheveningen. The **Paleis Noordeinde** is the official home of the monarch, and also in the suburbs is **Madurodam**, the model city (see page 111).

◆
**VOLENDAM, MONNICKENDAM, MARKEN**
Although a popular choice for the numerous coach companies operating out of Amsterdam, **Volendam** is a much over-rated town even though it does give the chance to see fishermen wearing baggy black pants and clogs and women starched lace. Pop in and take a short visit – there are only a couple of spots to look for and along the quay you will see the boats and the tackle, and the rather self-conscious residents. Not for the discriminating – perhaps you would be better off trying **Monnickendam** which is close by and less visited yet has a decided atmosphere and a charm of its own. Both these places are a short distance from Amsterdam and can easily be visited in half a day (many tours are on offer around the Stationsplein in Amsterdam).

**Marken** is another very popular spot, much visited, but despite its crowded aspect it still has an intriguing air due to its isolated position on the open spaces of what was once the North Sea. The houses are painted and raised on piles or mounds. You can sometimes see national dress worn here too.

◆
**ZANDVOORT**
A beach resort near Haarlem which offers good sand and shallow sloping beaches with dunes in the background. There is a **national dune park** here for nature lovers, and the bulb fields stretch away to the south. A new casino has just opened.

## PEACE AND QUIET

### Wildlife and Countryside in and around Amsterdam
### Introduction

The Netherlands is one of the lowest-lying countries in Europe, with much of the land lying at or below sea level and, despite this rather precarious existence, it is also one of the most densely populated regions. Much of the remaining land which is not built on is devoted to farming, and this land-use comprises nearly half the total land area of the country.

Fortunately, much of the agriculture is not as intense as in other areas of Europe and many of the farming practices and methods actually benefit elements of the wildlife. In particular, breeding wading birds such as the black-tailed godwit reach very high densities in the grazing pastures around Amsterdam. This elegant bird is just one of the 150 species which regularly breed in Dutch pastures, dunes, woodlands and wetlands.

The Netherlands has an extensive coastline with both young and stabilised sand dunes within easy reach of Amsterdam. The proximity of the sea as well as the pastures and wetlands, makes this city an ideal base from which to explore the wildlife of this fascinating country.

### Woodland and Heathland

You do not have to travel far from Amsterdam to reach

*A black-tailed godwit. The beak of this wader is packed with sensory cells which enable it to track its prey in deep mud*

good areas of forest. For example, in the woods around Harderwijk, only 18 miles (30km) east of the city, you can find interesting birds such as black woodpecker and short-toed treecreeper, the latter being the only species of treecreeper found in the region.

By travelling further afield to the national park areas of De Hoge Veluwe and Veluwezoom, both north of Arnhem, you can reach more impressive areas of ancient forest interspersed with patches of heathland. The pine and birch woodland have a wide variety of fungi, especially in the autumn, and the birdlife is some of the richest in the whole country. Both black and middle-spotted woodpeckers can be seen and heard, and in spring golden orioles, redstarts and wood warblers add to the dawn chorus. Goshawks, although declining in numbers, are still often seen and if you visit the area early in the spring you may be lucky and see their impressive courtship display above the tree tops. While circling and soaring they are often mobbed by smaller birds and are sometimes joined by

*Sea holly likes to grow in the more sheltered areas of sand dunes. It usually flowers in July and August*

other birds of prey such as sparrowhawks and kestrels. As dusk approaches, a woodland walk can be a rather eerie experience as a chorus of nocturnal bird-song starts up. Nightjars, which nest among the heather, churr all night long and hunt for insects in the air, while woodcock fly over the clearings making their peculiar squeaking call, known as 'roding'. These dumpy waders nest among the fallen pine needles and branches, but their camouflage is so good that you will need a keen eye to spot them. It is almost impossible to flush them and they do not fly off until you are almost on top of them. Dusk is also a good time to look for the woodland mammals of the region. Both red and roe deer are likely to be seen. The latter often feed in pairs, their white rumps being conspicuous when they are alarmed. Wild boar also frequent the more extensive areas of forest, but are more often heard than seen; they are noisy feeders as they rustle through the woodland floor in search of buried food.

**Coastal Flowers**
Lying less than 18 miles (30km) away from the city, the nearest part of the North Sea coastline is an easy drive from Amsterdam. The storm-battered shores are richly endowed with sand dunes and exciting coastal flowers stretching all the way from the Hook of Holland to Den Helder and along the entire chain of the Frisian Islands.

Coastal flowers have to be highly specialised since they must withstand the constant salt spray carried by onshore winds. The salt and the wind itself have a profound dessicating effect upon the plants which is compounded by their growing on extremely well-draining soils. Occasionally they are even inundated by seawater, something which would kill most terrestrial plants.

For the plants that grow along the Dutch coast, the sand and shingle are not a stable environment. The wind is constantly shifting the sand, either burying the plants or exposing their roots. Consequently, most of the coastal plants grow quickly and have extensive root systems which not only give them anchorage but also help them acquire water. Their leaves are often fleshy and waxy to help resist the drying effect of wind and salt and even their seeds are specially adapted. Many are completely resistant to seawater and can float, being carried by the tides to suitable beaches.

One of the first plants to colonise the sand and shingle is sea rocket, which has subtle mauve flowers. It often grows with prickly saltwort, with its spiny-tipped succulent leaves, along the tideline of the highest spring tides. Above the tidelines, the plants often appear to be growing out of bare sand, but in reality they make use of the buried humus from previous strandlines. The beautiful, chamomile-like flowers of sea mayweed often grow in profusion along the strandlines.

Higher up the beach, the succulent leaves of sea sandwort often form low-growing carpets over stable areas of rock and sand, while yellow-horned poppy, with its bright yellow flowers and long seed pods, nods in the breeze. The aptly named sea holly, with its prickly leaves and bracts, is often common and, despite its appearance, is in fact an umbellifer, more closely related to hogweed than to the thistles it resembles.

## Mudflats

Within the protection of the natural sea defences formed by the Frisian Islands lies an extensive area of calmer water called the Wadenzee. As the sea retreats on a falling tide leaves extensive sandbanks and mudflats which at low tide cover an area of almost 1,000 square miles (2,600sq km). The mudflats are exceptionally rich in marine life with immense numbers of lugworms, ragworms, bivalve molluscs and other marine invertebrates. This bonanza inevitably attracts birdlife in abundance and tens, if not hundreds, of thousands of gulls, waders and wildfowl gather. The marine life of the mudflats not only supplies the breeding birds of the region but also attracts huge congregations of autumn migrants and wintering species, and supports feeders which specialise in everything

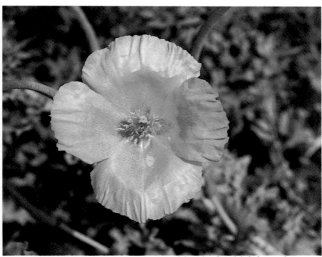

*Yellow horned poppy is one of the showiest of sand dune plants. It takes its name from its immensely long seed pods*

from invertebrates to fish. The waders are at their most impressive during late summer and autumn when dunlin, redshank, knot, grey plover, godwits and curlew are joined by less numerous species such as stints, greenshank and spotted redshank. When disturbed or when flying to roost, the vast wader flocks are an impressive spectacle. Common and black-headed gulls are always in attendance, hoping to supplement their diet with a meal stolen from an unfortunate wader.

The numbers of ducks and geese are also impressive on the Wadenzee. The most conspicuous species is the shelduck, a largely black and white duck which breeds on the dunes surrounding the mudflats and which feeds by filtering the mud for small molluscs. In autumn and winter they are joined by brent geese, which despite the size that their name implies, are no bigger than the shelducks. Their main food is eel-grass, which is dying out in the Wadenzee and hence adversely affecting the numbers of geese in the area. In the deeper channels and open water, mergansers, scoters and eiders dive for fish and marine molluscs.

Until recently, common seals were a feature of the Wadenzee and Frisian Islands. Their numbers are now sadly being depleted by a virus and it can only be hoped that they begin to develop an immunity before their numbers decline too far. If their populations

## PEACE AND QUIET

recover again the Wadenzee may once more be graced by the sight of these beautiful animals hauled out on sandbanks at low tide.

### Flevoland in Winter

Traditionally, winter has not been considered the best time of year to visit the Netherlands, but with the advent of bargain breaks, out of season trips are becoming more and more popular. Lying within easy reach of Amsterdam, Flevoland's polders, dykes and fields present an unrivalled spectacle for the birdwatcher with tens of thousands of geese, swans and ducks to be seen.

Flevoland's existence is due entirely to the efforts of man. It is an area of reclaimed land in the Ijsselmeer, itself formed in 1932 by the enclosure of the Zuiderzee. Because the process of reclamation is continuing all the time, polders of different ages occur with habitats ranging from mud to reedbed to established grazing pasture. This variety of habitats draws in all sorts of wetland birds.

Flevoland can be reached from Amsterdam itself or from several other access points. The land is criss-crossed by dykes which, in cold weather, provide a good elevated position from which to watch birds in the fields. Winter is the time for geese: white-fronted geese predominate with smaller numbers of pink-foots and bean geese. Occasionally greylags, whose numbers peak during their

August migration, linger on as well and for the keen observer there is always a chance of a rarity. Lesser white-fronted, red-breasted and snow geese occur almost annually, the latter, with its snow-white plumage, being the most conspicuous of the three. Thousands of Bewick's swans also visit Flevoland, sometimes joined by whoopers. Individual birds can be tricky to identify,

*These Bewick's swans are among the thousands upon thousands of birds that make Flevoland a birdwatcher's paradise in winter*

but side-by-side the whooper is much the larger of the two, and its larger bill shows more yellow. Flocks of swans are often joined by smaller wildfowl, and pintail, wigeon and pochard are common. The first 'skeins' of geese appear in the autumn and numbers build up to a maximum by January. If it is a mild winter then the numbers may be low, the birds having remained further north. However, if the temperatures suddenly drop then there will be an influx of geese and swans as they head south. If Flevoland itself becomes trapped in severe weather then the flocks often desert the fields and head for southern and western Europe, and England in particular.

**Grazing Pastures**

Much of the agricultural land around Amsterdam is used as grazing pasture and lies on ancient polders, many of which are actually below sea level. With the constant threat of inundation, the water levels have to be maintained and so

## PEACE AND QUIET

the familiar windmill landscape has developed. Nowadays, however, much of the windmill's work has been taken over by electric pumps. There are fine meadows all around Amsterdam, some of which are even within the city boundaries. However, a short drive north from the city to Waterland or south to Biesbosch near Rotterdam will reveal a greater variety of wildlife.

Because the grazing pastures are composed mainly of grass,

*Pastures and ditches such as these in Friesland make fine habitats for many species of bird, especially waders*

the vegetation is rather uniform and not of any special botanical interest. However, celery-leaved crowfoot, which seems to thrive where trampled and grazed, is conspicuous along muddy field margins and ditches. By contrast, the birdlife is extraordinarily varied and some species breed at higher densities here than anywhere else in Europe.

Black-tailed godwits are noisy and conspicuous residents of the pastures. These long-billed, long-legged waders nest in grassy tussocks and are frequently seen perching on fence-posts. These provide excellent look-outs over the fields and are used by other ground-nesting birds of the area (redshank, snipe and oystercatcher, for example) to survey their territories.

March and April see the arrival of a colourful little migrant from southern Europe and Africa. In this part of Europe the yellow wagtail occurs as a blue-headed race and dazzling males can be seen in aerial battles which help settle territorial disputes. Yellow wagtails are only summer residents, however, and are on their way south by September.

Black terns are one of the most elegant birds to nest in the fields around Amsterdam. Their buoyant flight allows them to catch insects on the wing and they hover and glide over open water, occasionally diving in to catch a small fish. Although their plumage is a beautiful sooty-black at the start of the breeding season, by July it has become worn and patchy making them look rather moth-eaten.

## Texel

The magical island of Texel is southernmost in the Frisian chain and is renowned throughout Europe for the variety and numbers of birds that it holds. It is within easy reach of Amsterdam, and although small in area, has a wide variety of habitats and 19 nature reserves.

Sand dunes face the North Sea gales and behind them pine woodlands help establish a stable soil system. Grazing fields, lakes and marshes all add to the interest of Texel. Although some of the island is closed for the summer to protect nesting birds, plenty can still be seen from the roads and areas of public access.

The dunes have an excellent variety of flowers, with sea rocket and sea holly abundant along the shore. Inland, marram grass helps establish the dunes and large colonies of common and black-headed gulls and terns nest in the shelter of the dune slacks. Kentish plovers are a speciality of Texel, having disappeared from most other areas of northern Europe, and long-since ceased to breed in the English county which gave them their name.

Here and there, eiders sit tight on their eggs, relying on their camouflage to avoid detection, while shelducks use abandoned rabbit burrows to rear their broods. Where pines have been planted or have become established, golden orioles and icterine warblers nest. Long-eared owls are also here but are difficult to see. Look for the tell-tale whitewash of droppings at the base of a tree and then scan the branches for the motionless owl.

Many of Texel's lakes are reed-fringed and have a rich variety of aquatic life, which in turn provides food for many wading birds such as avocet and spoonbill. The latter is another speciality of the island and parties are often seen flying overhead. Herons stalk the shallows and marsh harriers quarter the reedbeds, while in autumn, migrant waders like wood sandpiper and spotted redshank feed and build up their energy reserves.

The grazing pastures on Texel have all the species of wader found elsewhere in the Netherlands. Black-tailed godwits, redshank, snipe and oystercatcher are all common and crakes and rails lurk in the ditches. During the autumn and winter, the meadows play host to flocks of wildfowl, especially at high tide, and wigeon and brent geese can be numerous.

## Lakes

The west of the Netherlands is fortunate in having plenty of lakes, some of which are within easy reach of Amsterdam. To the north, the Zwanenwater lies on the route to Texel and is a coastal dune lake, while to

## PEACE AND QUIET

the south, Nieuwkoop is large and reed-fringed.

Depending upon the age and size of the lakes, they will have varying mixtures of aquatic plants and animals and ones with extensive reedbeds are often important nesting sites for birds. If they have been established for a long time, a good fish population will have developed with big ruffe, perch and pike being active predators.

The thriving fish populations support a wealth of fish-eating birds which nest around the lake margins. To avoid competing directly for food, each species of bird feeds in a slightly different way. Cormorants and black-necked grebes both dive in order to catch their food, but the former catches much larger fish than the latter. Bitterns prefer to wade in the shallows and wait for a fish to swim within range. These large waterbirds are more frequently heard than seen, the males 'booming' in the springtime to advertise their territories. Their diminutive relative, the little bittern, about the size of a moorhen, also haunts the reedbed margins of many lakes. Although rather shy, they are sometimes seen flying over the reeds when their pale wing panels make identification easy.

Some of the lake birds feed only on water plants, while others have a more mixed diet. The red-crested pochard, for example, dives deeply and takes aquatic vegetation from the bottom but supplements its diet with small fish, tadpoles and insects. Insects above the water's surface serve as food for a whole range of other birds. Swallows and martins hawk the lakes in search of midges and mosquitoes and are joined at dusk by swifts and black terns.

### Polders

The process of enclosing the sea, draining the water and

*Bitterns spend most of their time lurking among reeds, but sometimes they step into the open, revealing wonderful, cryptic plumage*

reclaiming the land has been going on for centuries in the Netherlands and much of the existing countryside would have been under the sea even a hundred years ago. The enclosed land is known as a 'polder' and the process continues today with the most notable examples being found on the ever-growing Flevoland.

After the water has been drained from the land, the ground is seeded with reeds to stabilise the soil. The variety of wetland habitats that are formed as a result, although only temporary, attracts all sorts of wildlife and makes important areas for breeding birds. On the open ground, common terns and avocets make their nest scrapes, while older reedbeds are the haunt of bearded tits. These delightful little birds look rather like feather dusters with their plump, round bodies and long tails. Their explosive, high-pitched calls have earned them the nick-name 'pingers' and after hearing them it is not difficult to understand why.

## PEACE AND QUIET

Bearded tits weave their nests among the stems of the reeds and share this habitat with reed and great reed warblers. Both these species are marvellous songsters as they cling to the highest reed stems. Dense reedbeds provide perfect cover for nesting marsh harriers, shy birds which are easily disturbed. Although scarce in most of Europe and persecuted in some regions, they are common here and the wealth of small birds and mammals ensures a good success rate for their young.

As succession takes place in the polders, meadows replace the reedbeds and small mammals move in to feast on the grass roots and shoots. Both short-tailed and ground voles can reach plague proportions and inevitably attract large numbers of birds of prey. Day-hunting short-eared owls and hen harriers quarter the ground and often stay to breed. During the winter months, rough-legged buzzards supplement their numbers and take a great toll on the voles. The polders of the Netherlands are possibly the best place in Europe to see these graceful raptors and up to 100 in a day can be seen on Flevoland alone in a good year. Even at a distance, they are easy to identify because they have a conspicuous white rump and a habit of hovering, an unusual feat for so large a bird.

### Marshes

Despite the managed nature of much of the countryside around Amsterdam, in some areas, wetlands have developed into superb marshes. Gnarled willows and tangled wetland undergrowth provide cover for secretive birds and mammals and many species nest here.

In some areas, such as Biesbosch near Rotterdam, the trees support breeding colonies of night herons. As their name suggests, they are nocturnal, spending the day roosting in the trees, and flying out at night to feed in the pools, lakes and ditches.

Although fish are important in the diets of most of the species of heron and bittern, amphibians are also frequently caught. Two of the commonest species are pool and edible frogs, which can be very difficult to distinguish and sometimes hybridise to confuse the issue. Both are very vocal, and like to sit about during the day basking in the sun's rays.

Where they are not disturbed or polluted, ditches and canals have an interesting variety of emergent water plants such as flowering rush and branched bur-reed. If sufficient cover develops, the ditches become the haunt of the shy water rail. Although they prefer to breed in extensive reedbeds, outside the breeding season water rails are found in all sorts of watery places, and ditches are a favourite winter site unless they freeze over.

Water rails are secretive birds, but give their presence away with their loud, pig-like

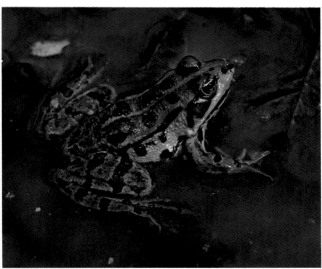

*Pool frogs are common marshland residents. They form a substantial part of the diet of such birds as herons and bitterns*

squeals. If you hear this sound then sit quietly beside the ditch or pool and wait: sooner or later the bird will emerge from cover. If you lose patience, try making a squeaking sound with a blade of grass because this sometimes fools the bird into thinking there is a rival in the vicinity and it temporarily forgets its natural shyness. Where marshes grade into managed flood meadows this provides a perfect habitat for ruffs. In the breeding season the male birds develop large, feathery 'ruffs' which are used in displays to other males, and, of course, to the females – which lack the head-dress. The 'ruffs' may be white,

brown or black and are lost outside the breeding season. The ritual display arenas, known as 'leks' are often on grassy knolls close to wet meadows and are used year after year.

**Birds of the Coast**
The extensive coastline of the Netherlands is very attractive to birds. There is something to see all through the year with breeding birds in the summer, migrants in spring and autumn and winter specialities along the beaches.
During the summer months, the coasts teem with vast numbers of breeding terns and gulls. Herring, black-headed and common gulls all form noisy colonies and sometimes are joined by nesting terns. Sadly, little and sandwich terns are no longer numerous, but

## PEACE AND QUIET

common terns form large colonies, laying their camouflaged eggs in shallow scrapes in the sand and shingle. The young are also extremely well camouflaged and are difficult to spot, and are consequently very vulnerable to disturbance and trampling by tourists.

All the terns catch fish and can be seen diving even into shallow water after sand eels and other small species. In the autumn, they leave Europe to migrate south for the winter, often flying in the company of other seabirds like shearwaters and skuas. These species, which spend most of their lives far from land, are most frequently seen during periods of onshore gales in September and October.

The coastal flowers provide shelter and food for invertebrates like grasshoppers and spiders. These animals, along with the seeds of the flowers, provide food for small birds. Tawny pipits and crested larks creep among the clumps of marram grass and sea holly, and along the strandline feeding as they go. During the autumn this same food supply revives tired migrants on their way south. September and October can witness huge 'falls' of songbirds, with flocks – hundreds or thousands strong – of bramblings, twites and snow buntings. At this time of year there is always a chance of an unusual bird coming in with one of these flocks. Bluethroats and barred warblers are regularly seen,

looking most out of place among the maritime plants. Some of the snow buntings stay for the winter and may be joined by shore larks. While shore larks creep around slowly and are sometimes difficult to see, the flocks of snow buntings burst into the air with jingling calls and flashing white patches on their wings.

### Bulb Fields

From March to May, the fields around Amsterdam become a kaleidoscope of colourful flowers. These are the famous bulbfields. Some of the best areas in the country lie between Leiden and Haarlem, within easy reach of the city. A day's driving along the dykes overlooking the bulbfields is a memorable experience.

Bulbs act as underground 'food stores' for many different plants – the most famous being tulips – and give the plants a 'head-start' over herbaceous plants, allowing them to flower much earlier. Also flowering in the early spring are the fruit trees, whose pink and white blossoms are a subtle contrast to the sometimes gaudy bulb flowers.

If you make a spring visit to see the bulb fields, be sure not to miss the gardens at Keukenhof, near Lisse. They are an easy drive from Amsterdam and are among the largest flower gardens in the world. In the 70 acres (28 hectares) of land, 6–7 million bulbs are reckoned to be planted each year – so it is no wonder that the gardens are a riot of colour in the spring!

*Schiphol Airport's duty free shops are extensive and for certain items may be better than the shops in central Amsterdam*

## SHOPPING

Shopping in Amsterdam can be divided into two parts – the city and the airport. You can do very well with certain items at Schiphol, so it is probably worth checking on what is available there before you splash out in the city centre. In the central city everything is in easy walking reach and offers possibilities for all purses from luxury to budget. There are major department stores selling all the smart items of clothes, records, perfumes, jewellery, linens and china (much specifically Dutch so of interest to tourists, but of course many imported goods too for the local market) and also hundreds of small speciality shops. The main streets are the two long thoroughfares, the Kalverstraat and the Nieuwendijk, and the Leidsestraat with its small shops mingled with cafés and also a walking street, although the trams and bikes whoosh down it so do not cross without looking first!

Appropriately for a city which has always been a trading centre, Amsterdam is a producer of many things, but most notable commodities are flowers and bulbs, diamonds, agricultural products, vegetables, cheeses and chocolate as well as handicraft items from woven blankets to wooden clogs, furniture and pottery. Luxury goods include fashion items and furs, pictures and sculptures, and antiquities – there is a special area of the city for fashion (around the

Museumplein) and for antiques (the Rokin and the Spiegelgracht).

## Books

Main area around the university district off the Spui and the Leidsestraat. Not all books are in Dutch – there are foreign language sections and English is well represented both in new and old bookstores. You are usually very welcome to browse.

**Book Market**: An interesting excursion can be made to the book market on the street known as the Oudemanhuispoort. Small secondhand shops, stalls and tables piled with volumes make this little street a fascinating place to visit on a sunny day.

**American Discount Book Centre**, Kalverstraat: A large store with many English volumes, a typical sort of cut-price place, breezy and modern. There is a so-called English tea-room here, Lindsay's, for a break between browsing, or to examine purchases.

**Athenaeum**, 3, NZ Voorburgwal: A longstanding shop, well-known in the city with interesting architectural features distinguishing its corner site – note the sinuous art nouveau window frames. Helpful staff. A pleasant sitting area close by is near the little statue of a backstreet Amsterdam boy known as 'the cheeky lad'.

Also on NZ Voorburgwal are antique and old books at number 304, and in a very

leaning old house at number 330.

**Erasmus**, Rokin: One of the city's most famous antique bookshops, with high quality collectors' items, but also affordable volumes.

**Newspapers and Magazines** (in English and other languages): A variety can be found near the station, at 34 Damrak.

## Bulbs

You can find them in all sorts of small shops (try shopping

*Cheese is a staple part of the Dutch diet, often eaten at breakfast. It is sold packaged in pieces or, better, whole*

along the cluttered streets around the Harlemmerdijk) or in the big stores and also at the airport. It might be best to save your bulb shopping until you make an excursion to one of the bulb-growing towns outside Amsterdam. Bulbs are sold in sacks, in paper envelopes, and loose and you may find that they can vary a lot in quality from place to place, so shop around.

**Airport Duty Free**, Schiphol: Not much on offer, but there are bulbs for sale, usually in small packs. You probably won't save much, but still useful for last minute presents.

**Flower Market**, The Singel: Here in a series of stands and flat bottomed boats moored on the canal you can buy a variety of bulbs as well as plants and flowers. They can be packed in bags, by the hundreds or by tens, and this is much the cheapest place to buy bulbs, since terms are cash only as a rule. Plenty to choose from, helpful and knowledgeable owners.

## Cheeses
You will taste a lot of Dutch cheese on a holiday – it is even part of typical Dutch breakfasts with cold meats.

## SHOPPING

You can find it packaged at any supermarket or food speciality shop, but it is best to buy a whole cheese, especially some of the aged Goudas, which are not easily obtainable outside Holland. Best way to get a cheese is at some of the cheese-towns around Amsterdam – Alkmaar, Edam and Gouda have markets and plenty of possibilities for shopping in their centres. (*Note*: there is a Cheese Museum at Alkmaar.)

### Chocolate

There is an abundance of small chocolate shops in the city, and their sales windows can be a joy, piled with hand-made chocolates, chocolate bars, chocolate packed in Delft tile designs, marzipan animals. Try the Leidseplein for little shops. Department stores have large sections, usually on the ground floor.

### Kwekkeboom

Reguliersbreestraat: Busy crowded store on a major street, filled with all kinds of pastries and rich chocolates.

**Pompadour**, Huidenstraat 12: An old-fashioned shop with a well-filled window. The place looks more like a salon than a chocolate shop, all articles are handsomely set out, and there is plenty to choose from.

**Airport Duty Free**: Plenty of choice, often special sales, from speciality shops on the main duty-free concourse. Few loose chocolates but lots of boxes and bars. Airport shops also accept credit cards.

### Coffee

Dutch coffee is rich and redolent. It is usually drunk fairly strong and the taste may not be yours, yet it is still worth looking into the Amsterdam coffee shops if only for the wonderful atmosphere and aroma of blends. Teas are also sold in the coffee shops as well

*There is plenty of opportunity for browsing in antique shops, though genuine old Delftware and tiles command huge prices*

as machines for making coffee, etc.

**Wijs Koffie**, 102 Warmoesstraat: Brass-framed windows and ornate old letters tell you this is a real old-established shop, full of age and charm. The scent of the coffee seems to have seeped everywhere. You can buy it loose or ready weighed in packets.

**Geels and Co**, 67 Warmoesstraat: Another old-timer, and a must even if you only look in the windows. Helpful in suggesting blends you may like. Modern aids for coffee-making sold. Old tins and implements to look at.

### Crafts/Antiques

Again, Dutch interest in crafts is evident in many small shops and galleries and antiques are sold from small cluttered shops in the older districts.

**Antiques de Loodier**, Elandsgracht: An antique market with many small stalls, a good introduction under one roof to what the city offers to collectors or just to curio seekers. Open from 11.00 to 17.00 every day except Wednesdays, free entry.

**Kiek's Horloger**, 206 Kalverstraat: Old clocks as well as modern timepieces in a very charming old shop illuminated with chandeliers.

**Muntplein 208**: Just one of many small hole-in-the-wall shops, with a good selection of glassware and jewellery.

**Dutch Arts and Crafts Centre**: Numerous stands and boutiques under one roof at the centre at Nieuwendijk, which is open every day except for certain Wednesdays out of the main season. An entrance fee is charged, but once in you can stay as long as you like and besides the many shops there are also studios where you can observe the crafts people at work on pots, jewellery, glassware, weaving, leatherwork, carving and fabric design. All places offer their wares for sale, and a friendly atmosphere prevails so feel free to ask questions.

### Department Stores

Not many big stores in the city, though there are several small ones and open-plan shops along the main shopping streets. International chain stores for shoes, clothes, fashions and foodstuffs can be found here also.

**Bijenkork**, Dam Square: De Bijenkork literally means 'the beehive' and it can be as busy as that on a Saturday or during its sales. Several floors offering everything from luxuries to staples. Look for Dutch handi-crafts here.

**Bonneterie**, Maison de la, 183 Kalverstraat: One of those hold-overs from an earlier age, this gracious shop is small yet smart with an old-style façade, specialising mostly in fashions.

**Esprit**, Spui: A modern store, small yet welcoming, with clothes and specialities, also a convenient and welcoming coffee bar, in the middle of the student section.

**Metz**, Keisersgracht 455: A general store in the centre of the city (off the Leidsestraat)

## SHOPPING

*Wandering round flea markets is a popular Dutch pastime for all the family. Haggling with stallholders is part of the fun*

with several floors. Wide variety of goods and a cheap, well-appointed snack bar.

### Diamonds

Even if you do not want to buy (and apparently there are bargains to be had) you will want to see the stones being cut and prepared in the workshops which can be found all over central Amsterdam. Entry is almost always free and you may even get free coffee too. Tours are on offer seven days a week but vary. Amsterdam has particularly skilled diamond cutters and the term 'Amsterdam cut' means top quality work. The Depression came down with particular force on the gem industry and then World War II meant many factories were closed or moved abroad because of the industry's many Jewish owners and skilled workers. After the war factories were concentrated in the centre – it is a clean non-polluting business – in order to be close to customers and the increasing tourist business. Many sales are now made direct to visitors, particularly the Japanese. A fascinating visit can be made with a tour guide giving a good, well-delivered talk on how diamonds are mined, cut and polished, and how quality is judged as regards size, colour and clarity. Seeing the craftsmen at their benches cutting the precious stones is also intriguing.

**Amsterdam Diamond Centre**, 1–5 Rokin: One of the biggest of the diamond cutters and polishers. Slick tours around this modern operation tend to be well run, but can be crowded and commercial.

**A van Moppes and Zoon**, 2–6 Albert Cuypstraat: This is one of the largest and most international of the companies, open every weekday. Near the museum section. You get a detailed tour and a look (through a microscope) at the tiniest cut-diamond known.

**Coster Diamond**, corner Paulus Potterstraat behind Rijksmuseum: A smart mansion is the setting for diamond-viewing here, and they may ask for an identity check. Open seven days a week from 09.00 to 17.00.

**Holshuysen-Stoeltie**, Wagenstraat (off Amstelstraat): This small and unprepossessing firm is one of

*The city's reputation for cutting and polishing diamonds is well-founded, and many visitors enjoy bargain-hunting*

the nicest in the city. Signs are in English and the informative tour lasts about half an hour. Diamonds have been an industry in the Dutch capital since the 17th century, and one room is set up as a museum with authentic tools and a diamond mill of the period. It is very interesting to compare this with the new methods on show. After you have gazed at the sparklers in the showrooms upstairs you are invited for a free coffee at their own small coffee house across the street. Not far from this factory is another, simply labelled 'Diamonds' at 209 Amstel.

**Flea Markets**
Local markets are very

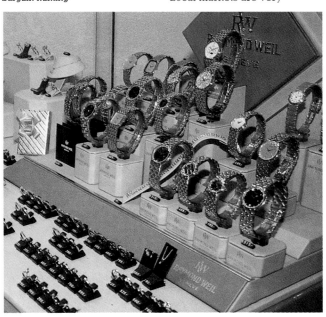

# SHOPPING

popular with the Dutch – they take the children and make it an outing. Lots of stalls and spaces, a vast mixture of things on sale from worthwhile antiques and furnishings to absolute rubbish. Second-hand clothes and video material. The food stalls are good: you can get all sorts of fast-food. It's well prepared – try the crisp chips with mayonnaise, Belgian style. Wander about with the crowd and enjoy the experience and the atmosphere.

**Albert Cuypmarkt**: One of the biggest and most expansive in Holland. Stalls are all along the Albert Cuypstraat off the Hobbemakade or approach via the Ruysdaelstraat. The streets round here, not far from the museum section, are all named after famous Dutch artists. Very much a local market with all sorts of foodstuffs as well as second-hand and new clothes. A good place too for a snack or a light lunch. The market also overflows into the Ferdinand Bolstraat which crosses it. Open early, the market is finished by 17.00 and everyone is packing up.

**Bird Market**: Around the Noorderkerk in the Jordaan on Saturday mornings. Cage-birds but also other items are on sale on Saturday mornings in the little square next to the church. The market extends down a local street, very much a neighbourhood place.

**Books**: second-hand volumes at Oudemanhuispoort, open Monday to Friday.

**Flower Market**: Beside the Singel, in the centre of town. Bulbs, plants, seeds and blooms.

**Nieuwmarkt**: A square that used to be a regular market, now open and tranquil – very different from wartime days when it was a centre of black-market business. There is an open-air antiques market here from spring to autumn, Sundays only. On the Thorbeckeplein off the Amstelstraat there is an art market, April–October, Sunday afternoons.

**Stamp and coin market**, for specialist interests. The rather dreary Nieuwezijds Voorburgwal is enlivened on Wednesdays and Saturday afternoons with dealers and collectors.

**Waterlooplein**: Beside the Muziektheater, a large and busy space which has been created for this Amsterdam institution after it was moved away for a period. It lacks character in its surroundings, yet is still a lively place filled with people looking at the stands and stalls. All sorts of stuff on sale, many clothes stalls, records and videos, knick-knacks, so-called antiques (mostly junk but of course you may see a treasure). Stall-holders can be pleasant, but also surly and sometimes rude. The food stalls are good, and cheap. Wander about munching a sausage, chips or a hamburger as the Dutch do. Even if you don't buy, it's fun. Beside the Jodenbreestraat, this is one market not to miss. Open weekdays.

## FOOD AND DRINK

### Eating Out

There are plenty of places to eat in Amsterdam, all the way from simple cafés to expensive restaurants with lush décors. There is a wide range of cooking styles, however, from the plain and filling Dutch dishes to Oriental, Greek, American, Mexican, Italian, Egyptian, Indian and Indonesian food. You have plenty of choice, and many places take credit cards and travellers' cheques. Restaurants often serve a Tourist Menu which is fixed at a set price each year. It is available at over 500 participating restaurants in Holland, and is marked with a special sign in blue of a fork between the words 'Tourist Menu'. It is often created

*All fish is fresh and very good. Smoked eels are a local delicacy not to be missed*

especially by the chef, and may well feature seasonal specialities. A leaflet listing all the participating restaurants is available from Netherlands Board of Tourism offices, and also from local tourist board offices in Holland. Wine tends to be dear, and so are drinks in smart bars. They are much more reasonably priced in unprepossessing local cafés. Dutch food is filling and sometimes heavy, with a strong accent on stews of meat or fish with vegetables, as well as hearty soups – pea soup (*erwtensoep*) being a favourite winter warmer, properly made with a hambone or bacon if you are lucky – accompanied by hunks of crusty bread. Fish is always popular and the nearby North Sea still provides a catch, as do local waterways for eels and freshwater fish. Fish is preserved in a number of ways from smoking to salting – try a pickled herring from a corner stand if you can find

## FOOD AND DRINK

one. Lots of poultry and eggs are eaten, and red meat grilled or fried. Main dishes are accompanied by mounds of vegetables and loads of potatoes, often fried. You can round off a typical Dutch meal with a large portion of good apple pie and ice cream. What Dutch food lacks in subtlety, it certainly makes up for in substance!

Sandwich bars can be found all over the city and are ideal for a light lunch in the middle of a day spent discovering the town. The sandwiches are called *broodjes* and are sometimes hot (*warme*). They can be on crisp white or brown bread, or on rolls both hard and soft. Wandering round markets you find many small stands selling things to eat, from fish and bread to cakes and fried potatoes. In summer people sit out with picnics on the wooden benches in certain squares and gardens.

The Dutch have a sweet tooth, so other items for immediate eating are the fluffed up *poffertjes*, the Dutch answer to doughnuts and quite delicious, as well as various cakes and pancakes, which are rolled up and filled with creams and jams (and can also have cheese or meat fillings as a main course). The chocolate and sweet shops are wonderful just to look at, and serve a variety of chocolates and goods made of marzipan. Dutch chocolate is very good and rich.

Dutch coffee is hot and strong, usually freshly made. For breakfast in hotels you will

*An Indonesian rice-table, popular with the Dutch whose connection with Indonesia dates back to 300 years of colonialism*

usually be offered coffee or tea (or hot chocolate) and then a range of cold meats and cheeses, or scrambled eggs, sausages, bacon at some places. There will be plenty of breads, and (increasingly) wholefood cereals with dried fruit and nuts, as well as a range of yoghurts. You can often fill up on a big breakfast and then not bother to eat again apart from snacks until the evening.

Indonesian food is much appreciated and it comes to Amsterdam through earlier colonial connections – many Indonesians settled in the city after the one-time colonies became independent. You certainly should try an exotic rice table (*rijsttafel*) with its many dishes and pile of rice to eat with them, and you will also get *satay* or skewers of meat chunks which have been prepared in peanut oil. The dishes are very varied and are not usually too highly spiced. As with Indian food it is probably best to drink a light Dutch beer with this kind of a meal, since wine rarely goes well with such strong and unusual flavours.

Cheap sandwich joints abound in central Amsterdam with hamburger chains in all the major streets – fast, filling and very popular with teenagers and children. Hardly adventurous but useful if you are in a hurry or do not really care what you eat. Department stores and museums have good quality cafeterias that are inexpensive. Those on a

budget might prefer to try a pizzeria – you can find them in central streets usually tricked out like an Italian restaurant, so the atmosphere is not as plastic as the American-style cafés. Wine is served and a whole pizza, with salad and the trimmings, plus drinks should not be more than Fl 22 for two and you will not be hurried out, so you can linger over your coffee (which is cheap in most places in Amsterdam). You may also want to explore less expensive snack-type restaurants and these can be found in department stores (such as Metz, Keisersgracht 455, 5th floor) or along central streets (try Berkhoff, Leidsestraat 46, or Pompadour, Huidenstraat 12) or you can try traditional light dishes such as pancakes at the Pancake Bakery, Prinsengracht 191, where you will find dozens of varieties of the *pannekoeken*. If you are a vegetarian then Holland welcomes you with plenty of possibilities, from buffets offering mounds of salads, to speciality restaurants. Oriental and Indian restaurants will often have vegetable dishes. Kosher food can also be found. If you want special foods then it is wise to check before going to Holland for a list of places from the tourist offices, or ask at the VVV when you arrive.

### Drinking

The traditional place to drink in Amsterdam is at the 'brown bars' (named for the tobacco which seems to have invaded the very woodwork of some of

## FOOD AND DRINK

*Café society is relaxed, friendly and caters for all tastes*

the older ones, leaving a dark brown patina). These can be found all over the city, often crowded with local people at busy times such as the end of afternoon, but usually friendly. As in Germany, brewing of beer is a national skill. There are big breweries in the city; one of the largest is Heineken's, on the Stadhouderskade. The competitor, Amstel, is almost as large and you will see advertising signs for the two brews all over the country as well as other less well-known ones. Bars will sell beers either in bottle or on tap with the latter being cheaper. Beer is sometimes drunk with Genever gin, the Dutch variety of the spirit and very cheap at duty free areas and in shops if you happen to like the fiery taste. It does not lend itself well to mixes and is almost always drunk on its own in tiny tumblers.

Wine is obtainable easily in Amsterdam, but is better drunk in good quality restaurants with a good list. Wine bars are still rare, but you can find modern bars serving cocktails and beer, usually in stark designs and with loud music and discreet lighting. In general, a café or brown bar is more atmospheric. In summer people take their drinks outside and some of the bars have little terraces on the canals which make very pleasant places to stop and enjoy the local scene.

Coffee is an urban necessity in Amsterdam and almost anywhere will allow you to either sit at a table with a coffee or stand at the bar and just have a cup, fresh brewed and fragrant.

### Dutch Restaurants

The following all display the sign of the 'dis' – a red, white and blue soup tureen to show that here you can eat traditional Dutch cooking.

**Bodega De Keyser**, Van Baerlestraat 96 (tel: 711441). This 'bodega' is an Amsterdam institution. It is near the Concertgebouw and attracts patrons to its terrace and cosy café atmosphere. Go for a drink or for a meal, but you may need to book in the evening.

**De Roode Leeuw**, Damrak 93-94 (tel: 240396). Set close to the entertainment centre of the city, this restaurant specialises in solid Dutch food. Its reasonable prices help to make it popular with locals.

**Die Port van Cleve**, NZ Voorburgwal 178-80 (tel: 240047). A restaurant of atmosphere with wooden panelling and tile mural. This is a place to try old-style Dutch cooking with many special dishes such as the famed pea soup, stews, sauerkraut and boiled puddings.

**Visrestaurant 'Julia'**, Amstelveenseweg 160 (tel: 795394). A noted fish restaurant offering fresh as well as smoked and cured fish.

**Other Dutch restaurants combining other cuisines with Dutch dishes**

**De Groene Lanteerne**, Haarlemmerstraat 43 (tel: 241952). Very much a neighbourhood place, long and very narrow, 300-year-old room offering Dutch dishes and French cuisine as well.

**d'vijf Vlieghen**, (The Five Flies), Spuistraat 294 (tel: 245214). A famous old place this, a warren of rooms, rambling through several houses and with unusual period decors and much good old furniture and decorative items. Note the etchings, said to be Rembrandt originals. Expensive, but an experience. Dutch and French.

**Die Nachtwacht**, Theorbeckeplein 2 (tel:

224794). Right in the nightclub district near Rembrandtsplein, it is a smart place with many dishes featuring steak and sea foods. Reasonable.

**French**

**Beddington's**, Roelof Hartstraat 6 (tel: 765201). Decor at this cool, modern restaurant may at first appear a little austere, but there is always a warm welcome. The food is highly imaginative, cooking very competent, and presentation quite artistic. Booking essential.

**Hôtel de l'Europe, Excelsior Restaurant**, Nieuwe Doelenstraat 204 (tel: 234836). Situated right in the heart of Amsterdam, this elegant restaurant has superb views over the river Amstel, the flower market and the Munttoren. Impeccable service, old-world ambience, mainly classical French dishes prepared in an imaginative, quite modern style. There is an emphasis on seafood but the menu is well balanced.

**Tout Court**, Runstraat 17d (tel: 258637). Small and cosy, slightly bohemian. Excellent French cuisine bourgeoise. Loyal guests include musicians who come here to enjoy their favourite dishes after the evening's concert. Always crowded, so book well in advance.

**Garden Hotel, De Kersentuin**, Dijsselhofplantsoen 7 (tel: 642121). This is undoubtedly one of the most elegant restaurants in town. *Kersentuin* means cherry orchard, hence the slight Japanese touch as

## FOOD AND DRINK

well as the red cherry in the aperitifs and on the china. A slight Italian bias, so there is excellent pasta. The lounge often features modern art exhibitions, fashion shows, and other such events. Booking necessary.

**De Trechter**, Hobbemakade 63 (tel: 711263). Small and modest, this restaurant is now considered one of the best in Amsterdam. The decor is simple, the atmosphere cosy, and the quality of food outstanding. Speciality is smoked food. There are only eight tables so book well in advance.

**Christophe**, Leliegracht 46 (tel: 250807). A relatively new restaurant but already a great success. Situated on one of the small canals behind the Westerkerk in the Jordaan area (the old quarter of the town), this spacious restaurant is cool, comfortable, and tastefully decorated. The menu offers light and stylish cooking at surprisingly reasonable prices, and in generous portions. It's a very popular place and is often crowded after 21.00 so late diners should book well in advance.

### Health Food Restaurant

**Manna**, Spui No 1, near Kalverstraat.
More of a shop and snack bar, but worth noting for those who do not want a meat diet which often seems hard to avoid in hearty-eating Amsterdam. Centrally placed. The tables in the gallery offer a range of vegetarian cooking and there is a take-out service.

### Indian
**Koh-i-noor**, Westermarkt 29 (tel: 233133). This is a very good restaurant, centrally placed and deservedly popular. It suggests reasonably priced set menus as well as classic Indian dishes. Good portions and good value – hence it is usually busy so make reservations.

### Indonesian
**Speciaal**, Nieuwe Leliestraat 142 (tel: 249706). Indonesian food is one of the delights of Amsterdam, the many restaurants showing connections forged in the colonial era. This one is small,

*One of Amsterdam's numerous Indonesian restaurants*

a bit off the track, yet worthwhile and reasonable. **Padi Mas**, de Lairessestraat 87 (tel: 733141). A popular Indonesian restaurant within the Memphis Hotel, offering good food at reasonable prices. Within easy walking distance of the Concertgebouw, the van Gogh and Stedelijk museums and the Rijksmuseum.

### Mexican
**Rose's Cantina**, Reguliersdwarsstraat (tel: 259797). A fashionable place, since Mexican food is very modish with the young trendies of Amsterdam. It is also pretty authentic here, and cheap. Very crowded, expect to wait.

### Oriental
**Treasure**, NZ Voorburgwal 15 (Pekinese cooking) (tel: 234061). Chinese specialities include Pekinese food in this authentic restaurant which is not a cheap place to eat – rather the reverse, in fact. But good and well-prepared dishes.

**Dynasty**, Reguliersdwarstraat (tel: 268400). A most elegant, exotic restaurant: orchids, golden Buddhas, Thai silk hangings, a stylish little garden for dinner outside on fine summer evenings. Service is perfect, and the refined cooking features dishes of southeast Asia, Malaysian dishes and good classic Cantonese, Thai and Vietnamese food based on lobster, prawns, fish, lamb and pork.

## FOOD AND DRINK

### Seafood

**De Bols Taverne**, Rozengracht 106 (seafood and steaks) (tel: 245752). This is a stylish and popular restaurant, an old warehouse which is decorated throughout with a sea and sailing decor in its rooms. Naturally fish and seafood are the staples, but you can also get meat such as steak, and bar meals too.

**Lucius**, Spuistraat 247 (seafood and unusual desserts) (tel: 2413831). A very agreeable and cosy place this, with atmospheric interiors and a style of its own. Speciality is fish, with a large selection and moderately priced.

**Le Pecheur**, Reguliersdwarsstraat (tel: 243121). The setting evokes a 1920s Paris bistro at this simple but very good fish restaurant. The fish is outstandingly fresh and beautifully cooked, with interesting, light sauces. The restaurant is situated behind the flower market in a trendy street full of popular eating places, and in summer you can eat out in the small garden at the back.

### Outside Amsterdam

**De Bokkedoorns**, Zeeweg 53, Overveen (tel: (023) 263600). One of the best restaurants in the Netherlands, De Bokkedoorns stands in a peaceful lakeside setting of dunes and woodland about 15 miles (25km) from Amsterdam. Wonderful fresh food which varies according to seasons: morels from the dunes, grilled scallops, tender Dutch lamb and unusual game dishes.

Very good sweets too. There is an attractive light lunch menu and in summer you can dine on the terrace. Booking recommended, especially at the weekends.

**Bistro Klein Paardenburg**, Amstelzijde 59, Ouderkerk a/s, Amstel (tel: (02963) 1335). About 6 miles (10km) from Amsterdam, in a quiet village on the River Amstel, this small country inn offers marvellous food, combining a great deal of imagination with a classic touch. Salmon, Dutch lamb, seafood and fantastic salads. Homely sweets, outstanding Dutch cheeses. Very popular, so book well in advance.

**Molen 'De Dikkert'**, Amsterdamseweg 104a, Amstelveen (tel: 411378). De Dikkert (meaning the big one) is a majestic old windmill right in the middle of a village on the outskirts of Amsterdam. It forms the setting for this stylish restaurant, popular with the international business community (there's even a menu in Japanese). This is the place for the best Dutch products – veal and lamb, seafood and asparagus, oysters and smoked eel. An impressive wine list includes a good choice of half-bottles.

**Auberge De Nederlande**, Duinkerken 3, Vreeland (tel: 02943). Old country inn on the pretty shores of the river Vecht, where in the 18th century the rich merchants of Amsterdam built their mansions and summer houses. The menu is seasonal; the cooking light and very good. There's also a bistro.

*The range of accommodation is wide – from luxury hotels to basic youth hostels . . .*

## ACCOMMODATION

You will find in Amsterdam an amazingly wide variety of places to stay, from hotels of great luxury and style to cheap budget accommodation of shared rooms or dormitories. Many small and reasonable hotels are in the centre, clustered along the canals, concentrated in such areas as the Leidseplein. Many are in old houses, redolent with the Dutch charm of hanging plants, pottery and a cosy element of clutter. The Dutch passion for cleanliness is usually evident in sparkling brass, copper and glass and there is a definite air of homeliness. Old houses in the city, with their steep staircases, wide windows and cheerful neighbourliness are very pleasant places to stay, some of them with canal views.

Bedrooms may not be large in older places, but you can usually be sure of a very comfortable bed in a warm yet not overheated house with the personal attention of the owners from the time you check in.

The bigger hotels are scattered around the city centre and the airport. There is a wide selection and while expensive they are not as dear as in some other cities. Some are conventional chain-type hotels, others are unusual both architecturally and from a service point of view. (Note the Pulitzer and the American Hotel, both deservedly landmarks of hospitality in this city and well worth considering if you want something different at a luxury price.) Needless to say all take credit cards, and offer the usual range of top-class service. Some have particularly good places to eat and some are noted as being places to which stars and royalty are drawn. (Note the Amstel Hotel facing the river.) Anyone visiting Amsterdam will want to be in the middle, and you have a range of places to choose from in the centre. You may save money by staying in the suburbs, but usually the inconvenience is not worth the small saving. Package tour companies usually offer a variety of hotels. An excellent one is Travelscene, but you could also try Time Off or book through *Amsterdam, the Amsterdam Way*, a service of the National Reservations

## ACCOMMODATION

Centre (see below), and a winter-only deal. This can be checked out with the Dutch National Tourist Office or the VVV Amsterdam Tourist Office. It offers a range of hotels and a series of prices as well as a number of free items from canal cruises to museum entries and free drinks. The scheme usually operates from 1 November to 31 March and more information is available from the NRC itself.

In most hotels except the very expensive you will be provided with a typical Dutch breakfast, sometimes in buffet-style but often served to you at the table. It will always feature cold meats, thinly sliced cheese (Dutch of course), boiled eggs and a variety of breads and toasts. More and more hot dishes of eggs, bacon, sausage and ham are available, so you can make a full meal of your breakfast, which comes of course with strong coffee, tea or hot chocolate, and sometimes cereals, juices and yoghurts to start with. If you eat heartily you will not want to spend much time lunching, and this will give you added hours to sightsee. If your dinner is typical you will get hearty helpings – another good reason for making your

*The American Hotel, just off the Leidseplein, is in the deluxe class and with its Art Deco features is a city landmark*

lunches in Amsterdam light and sensible!
Do not automatically expect a private shower or bath in this city – ask if you do need private facilities, otherwise you may have to share a bathroom with a neighbour or two. This is not usually too inconvenient, but check when you book.

**Reservations**
Remember that in the summer, at Christmas and New Year, and during such busy tourist times as the tulip season (April–May), hotels can be very busy and you may not have a wide choice. Prices vary by season, but not usually by very much. It is always wiser to have accommodation booked ahead at busy periods, if only for your own peace of mind. Amsterdam does have a high rate of turnover, however, so you will usually be accommodated even if it does mean waiting around sometimes.

**VVV Accommodation service**
This is intended for people who are already in the country and need assistance in finding accommodation. VVV offices (there are more than 90 of them in Holland) offer a joint reservation for same-day bookings, either for a night or subsequent nights. From VVV offices outside Amsterdam bookings for accommodation in the city can be made by visiting the local office (not by telephoning) and suggestions will be made depending on availability. Reservations for accommodation can be made at any VVV office bearing the

sign 'i-Nederland' with a large and eye-catching lower case 'i'. Another service run by the VVV is a programme that introduces visitors to local families.

**The National Reservation Centre** (NRC) PO Box 404, 2260 AK Leidschendam (tel: 070 202500). A useful and efficient national booking service for all kinds of accommodation from leading hotels to typical Dutch log cabins in the country. Open from 08.00 to 20.00 Monday to Friday, Saturdays 08.00 to 14.00. Reservations are confirmed in writing.

**Hotels**
**American Hotel** Leidsekade 97 (tel: 6245 322), 4-star, 1st class, 188 rooms. A fine example of early 20th-century styles with red brick, stained glass, tiles and plaster decoration. The Café Americain on the ground floor is a landmark with geometrical lighting fixtures and reading tables littered with magazines and newspapers.
**Amsterdam Apollo** Apollolaan 2 (tel: 6735 922), 5-star, de-luxe, 217 rooms. Ultra modern, just beyond the centre, overlooking the water with café terraces, most rooms in low-rise block.
**Amsterdam Ascot** Damrak 95-98 (tel: 6260 066), 4-star, 1st class, 110 rooms. A new addition to the city's supply of hotels, the Ascot is very centrally placed near the Dam and is well designed with views from its front rooms in a modern canal-house style building.

## ACCOMMODATION

**Amsterdam Hilton** Apollolaan
138 (tel: 6780 780), 5-star, de
luxe, 274 rooms. A typical
Hilton, large and streamlined,
just beyond the centre. Wide
views.

**Amsterdam Marriott**
Stadhouderskade 21 (tel: 6835
151), 5-star de luxe, 395 rooms.
A handsome new construction,
well placed for the Leidseplein
and the museums.

**Amsterdam Okura** Ferdinand
Bolstraat 333 (tel: 6787 111),
5-star, de luxe, 385 rooms. As
its name implies, a Japanese
hotel beyond the central
district, on a canal.

**Amsterdam Sonesta** Kattengat
1 (tel: 6212 223), 5-star, de luxe,
425 rooms. A strikingly modern
hotel, well placed in a central
location on canals and within
easy reach of the main
shopping streets, craft centre
etc, surrounded by old canal
houses.

**Canal House Hotel**
Keizersgracht 148 (tel: 6225
182), 2-star 'comfortable' hotel,
27 rooms. A small yet perfectly
charming, old-style hotel with
antiques and an elegant air.

**Crest Hotel** De Boelelaan 2
(tel: 6462 300), 5-star, de luxe,
261 rooms. Near the Amstel,
yet quite a way from the
centre, this bold black block
surmounted with the name in
lights is a landmark. Handy for
drivers, and one of several
Crest holdings in the city.
Others are the modern
Caransa Crest, the stylish old
Doelen Crest, the Rembrandt
Crest, also elegant, and the
Schiller Crest. All these are
4-star, 1st class and all central.

**Digla Hotel** Keizersgracht

*The 17th-century Doelen Crest
Hotel claims to have been visited
by both Rembrandt and the Beatles*

37–39 (tel: 6249 600), 2-star, 16
rooms. A canal house, actually
a pair, with elegant plaster
gables and big windows,
overlooking the canal.

**Garden Hotel**
Dijsselhofplantsoen 7 (tel: 6642
121), 5-star, de luxe, 97 rooms.
Beside a water way near the

Known as the queen of
Amsterdam's hotels this is an
old-style grand hostelry.
Facing the wide Amstel, a little
out of the centre, yet
accessible, it is a favoured
place for local special events
and visiting dignitaries.
Terrace and a noble stone
stair in the foyer.
**Jan Luyken** Luykenstraat 58
(tel: 6764 111), 4-star, 1st class,
63 rooms. Just across from the
Leidseplein and handy for the
Vondelpark and museums, a
neat old-style place, some
rooms with balconies.
**Krasnapolsky, Grand Hotel**
The Dam 9 (tel: 65549 111),
4-star, 1st class, 370 rooms.
Originally a truly elegant hotel,
but now much of its air of class
has been sacrificed for a
modern look. Very central,
handy for all shops and
services.
**Maas Hotel** Leidsekade 91 (tel:
6233 868), 1-star, plain but
comfortable, 29 rooms. A
bargain type hotel, facing a
canal, not far from the centre
and quietly situated.
**Museum Hotel, AMS** PC
Hooftstraat 2 (tel: 6732 459),
3-star, very comfortable, 116
rooms. A medium priced hotel
on the edge of the museum
district, old-style classic looks.
**Pulitzer** Prinsengracht 315 (tel:
6228 333), 5-star, de luxe, 240
rooms. Quite simply a unique
place – it consists of a group of
canal houses cunningly
converted to make a hotel of
rare distinction. Every room is
different and beautifully
contrived. There are internal
courts and gardens and art
galleries too. If you are going

Apollolaan and handy for the
museums and the Vondelpark.
**Holiday Inn Crown Plaza** NZ
Voorburgwal 5 (tel: 6200 500),
5-star de luxe, 270 rooms. A
classic Holiday Inn interior and
modern throughout, yet placed
in the old centre and handy for
all services and shopping.
**InterContinental Amstel** Prof
Tulpplein 1 (tel: 6226 060),
5-star, de-luxe, 111 rooms.

## ACCOMMODATION

to town in Amsterdam, this is the place for you.

**Roemer Visscher** Roemer Visscherstraat 10 (tel: 6125 511), 3-star, very comfortable, 50 rooms. A usefully placed medium price hotel on a street near the museums.

**Weichmann Hotel** Prinsengracht 328 (tel: 6263 321), 2-star, comfortable, 28 rooms. A bargain hotel of character on a canal, furnished with antiques, quiet and central.

### Hostels

Hostels can be a good answer for those on a budget. There are several in Amsterdam run by various bodies but best-known are the Dutch youth hostel chain, the Stichting Nederlandse Jeugdherberg Centrale (NJHC), Prof Tulpplein 4, 1018 GX Amsterdam (tel: 264433). There are two hostels in Amsterdam itself, one at Kloveniersburgwal 97, the Stadsdoelen (open spring to autumn) and a large one at Zandpad 5, near the Vondelpark. They are not restricted to the young alone, and families and older people are welcomed provided they hold membership in their own country, or have an international youth hostel card. Rates are very low, with prices varying according to the category of accommodation. Cooking facilities are available in some hostels (there are about 50 youth hostels in Holland). The NJHC also concerns itself with group accommodation, programme and route planning for visitors.

For very cheap accommodation the Sleep-In, Mauritskade, is useful. Information and a bar too (tel: 947444).

### Boarding Houses

Family atmosphere and the chance to meet the Amsterdam people are the attractions of a stay in a Dutch boarding-house. You may find difficulty in locating these places which are basically bed-and-breakfast, but do also provide an evening meal as a rule. The main office of the VVV may refer you to local offices, and you will need to book ahead as this type of accommodation is limited, especially in summer.

### Self-catering

Self-catering houses and cottages on the outskirts of the city (and also some flats right in town) can be found for people who do not wish to stay in hotels. The tourist office should have details of such rentals, and cottage accommodation can also be booked through the NRC, but again for summer booking you will need to make reservations as early as possible. A large family, or group, can often find very favourable rates in rented accommodation, and if you choose carefully you can find places that are close to bus and tram connections into the city.

### Camping

Camping is allowed only on specific sites in Holland. You cannot spend the night in a camper or caravan in a parking lot or lay-by.

## AMSTERDAM BY NIGHT

There are scores of theatres in Amsterdam, most small and presenting anything from dance and mime to modern Dutch plays. There are occasional plays in English to be seen but most popular with foreigners are the ballet, the opera and the concerts of classical music. A new theatre is a landmark in Amsterdam now, the Muziektheater which opened its doors in 1986 and became the home of the opera and the National Ballet. These important companies give seasons, but the visitor might also try some of the small,

*The Rembrandtsplein is where it all happens at night. The square is lined with lively bars, clubs and restaurants*

almost pocket-size theatres that can be found all over Amsterdam. There is plenty of music to be heard in the city, and many visiting attractions. The centre for the thriving entertainment industry of Amsterdam is the Leidseplein which, as well as the massive Stadsschouwburg, is a centre for street artists and entertainers.

### Theatres/Concert Halls

**Concertgebouw** Museumplein. This is Holland's most famous concert hall, and presents an enormous number of concerts over the year, often with star instrumentalists and conductors. It is renowned for its fine acoustics. An impressive place with its bold 19th-century design, it is the home of the Concertgebouw

## AMSTERDAM BY NIGHT

Orchestra, the major Dutch classical orchestra. Not all concerts are expensive however: there is a series of free lunchtime concerts, usually Wednesdays at 12.30.
**Melkweg** off Leidseplein. This is more of a centre for alternative culture than just a theatre – there are many attractions housed under the 'Milky Way's' one roof. Here you will find pop concerts, 'happenings', alternative theatre, exhibitions and a café. Entry is normally by membership, but you can usually enter by day at the café entrance on the Marnixstraat. At night the scent of marijuana is often wafted on the air.

**Muziektheater** Waterlooplein. A striking development beside the City Hall (Stadhuis) on the Amstel, this ought to be visited if only just to stroll through its foyers (when there is no performance in progress). The main theatre is semi-circular and seats about 1,500. But the Muziektheater is more than just

*The Stadsschouwburg theatre, built at the end of the 19th century, houses the Dutch Public Theatre and national opera and ballet companies*

well served with trams and bus services – there is a large car park under the Muziektheater.
**Stadsschouwburg** Leidseplein. This big old-style theatre dominates one side of the square and its arcade is a home for all sorts of alternative entertainers. Plays, some opera and ballets are presented in the auditorium with its proscenium arch stage, making a stately setting for a special evening. Many international companies are presented here, but plays are usually in Dutch. The arcade in front of the theatre is popular with street entertainers who make this foot passage their headquarters.

### Dance
There are good dance companies in Amsterdam, both big and small, and the major ones have a high standing around the world, with a particular style fostered by native dancers and choreographers of very high calibre. You *can* see productions of the classical works, but most likely events are modern works of stark beauty, stressing the physicality and sheer ability of the human body to move in compelling ways. Dutch dance style can be surprising and innovative.
The Dutch National Ballet is a major company which gives regular seasons at the Muziektheater, its home base. This company presents both classical and modern ballet, while the Netherlands Dance Theatre, which occupied a

a theatre, it is a parade of places – restaurants, cafés, shops and a booking office for all events. It is home to the main national companies and there are also seasons by leading international companies, mostly opera and ballet. The nearby Waterlooplein has a handy Metro station and the centre is new theatre in the seat of government at The Hague, can be seen in works stressing contemporary origins and almost always originating within the company, although some works from abroad are incorporated in the repertoires of both groups. Both companies are top class and well worth getting to know. For the activities of smaller companies and individual dancers in Amsterdam, check entertainment listings or look for posters around the town, especially in the university area, or in the arcade in front of the Stadsschouwburg.

### Opera

The other resident company of the Muziektheater is the Netherlands Opera which shares the space and seasons with the ballet. Besides productions of major operatic works you can see experimental works, and these are often presented during the period of the Holland Festival, an annual event in June, which is a very good time for the arts lover to visit the city. The Netherlands Opera is a major company with full chorus and a complete orchestra, usually the Netherlands Philharmonic, and sometimes there are guest stars.

### Tickets

Tickets can be bought at the theatre itself (hours: Monday to Saturday from 10.00, Sundays from noon) or from the two offices of the VVV tourist information centres, or the AUB (Amsterdam Uitburo) which sells tickets for all major

events from its office on the Marnixstraat, just off the Leidseplein. VVV offices in other Dutch cities will book theatre tickets for you too. The city has over 14,000 performances of opera, music, ballet and theatre every year.

### Nightclubs, Bars and Cafés

There are many nightclubs and cafés where you can hear music, or individual singers. African music is popular, so also is jazz both classical and funk, and the clubs around the Rembrandtsplein are the places to find it. Most of these spots are open every night, some are weekends only, but the programmes usually start late and go on well into the

*Live music continues until the early hours in many of the city's bars, cafés and nightclubs*

small hours.

A walk along the Reguliersdwarsstraat will give you a sample of Amsterdam's nightlife. Cafés and bars usually stay open until 01.00 during the week and later at weekends, but nightclubs and cabarets will continue well into the small hours. The style is intimate, small and crowded and the variety on offer is very wide from the newest experiments in punk to old-style Latin music. Even neighbourhood bars will have a piano, whether a 'brown bar' or the newer style 'white bars' often done up in modern interpretations of Art Deco. These are popular with a younger crowd and so are the multi-media spots, noisy and brash yet good for finding out what's new. Amsterdam must be unusual in that its bars and clubs are friendly, there's little sense of the shady or underhand (if you discount the use of soft-drugs, which can seem unusual to the non-Hollander), and you are not likely to get ripped off or stuck with huge bills at the end of an evening.

Amsterdam also has clubs for gay men (notably at the Kerkstraat and along the Warmoesstraat close by the Dam Square, and on the

Reguliersdwarsstraat near the Muntplein) and also for lesbians. Information on meeting places and cafés is available from a useful central office and café on Rozenstraat called the COC, open Wednesdays to Sundays until 18.00. There are discos for the local community here and for visitors every Friday, Saturday and Sunday night until late.

### Bars

Almost all the principal hotels in the city will have bars (and they will be open most of the time) but for more atmosphere try the following:

**Bamboo Bar**, Lange Leidsedwarsstraat, for blues and jazz

**Cab Kaye's Jazz Piano Bar**, Beulingstraat 9, for songs to the piano

**Canecao**, Lang Leidsedwarsstraat 70, for

*Liberated life in Amsterdam: women dance the night away in one of several gay bars to be found in the city*

South American music

**Costes**, Rosmarijnsteeg 9, Oriental jazz from Japan

**Crest Hotel's Clock Bar**, de Boelelaan 2, piano bar

**De Ijsbreker**, Weesperzijde 23, very much a local Dutch place with unusual new music

**Joseph Lam Jazzclub**, van Diemenstraat 8, for Dixieland

**Jazzcafe Alto**, Korte Leidsedwarsstraat 115, traditional jazz

**Odeon**, Singel 460, disco with late night concerts

**Okura Hotel (Ciel Bleu)**, Ferdinand Bolstraat 175, piano bar

**The String**, Nes 98, folk and country music

### Cafés and Brown Bars

**American**, Leidsekade 97 in the American Hotel

**Gollem Bierakademie**, Raamsteeg 4

**Cafe Kolkhaven**, Westermarkt, very old well-preserved bar and café

**Hoppe**, Spui 18-20

**Melkweg Cafe**, Marnixstraat 47, media café popular with the young

**Papeneiland**, Prinsengracht 2, famous old brown café

**Henry's**, Rokin 89, an attempt at a British pub

**De Smoeshaan**, Leidsekade 90

**De Zeilvaart**, de Ruijterkade 106

Also try De Saloon, Eijders, Het Cafe.

### Dancing

**Boston Club** in the Sonesta, Kattegat 1

**Juliana's**, Apollolaan 138-140

**De Schakel**, Korte Leidsedwarsstraat 49

**Zorba**, OZ Voorburgwal 216

*Tulips herald the start of Holland's tourist season*

## THE WEATHER

Mild winters, cool summers. Driest times February to May. See chart, page 107.

## WHEN TO GO

Amsterdam will forever be associated with tulips and bulbs of every type, and of course the months of April and May bring in many visitors to see Holland's bulbfields. At any time of the year, however, Amsterdam is an ideal place to go to for a break.

## SPECIAL EVENTS

**January**
Antique shows

**February**
A carnival takes place each year with a large parade through the centre

## SPECIAL EVENTS

**March**
Rowing events on the River
Amstel.
Heineken Tournament
Car rallies
Boat show
Spring flower show at the Artis
Zoo (for exact dates ask at the
VVV Tourist Office in Holland
or, from abroad, check with
Dutch Tourist Office)
**April**
The lighting of various
important and interesting
architectural features of the
city starts, best viewed from
the water
The birthday of the Queen on
30 April is celebrated with
many events
**May**
A marathon centres on the
Dam Square
**June**
The Vondel Park has a series
of open-air performances
The International Royal
Holland Cup is rowed
The annual Holland Festival
takes places for the entire
month and occupies a number
of places around the city (early
reservation for major events is
necessary)
**July**
Carillon concerts from the
main churches in July and
August
Summer festival of the smaller
theatres
**August**
Open-air chess competition is
played on the Dam
**September**
Jordaan district has its own folk
festival
Antique car parade
Fashion designers show their
collections at Amsterdam

Mode Stad
The huge flower market at
Aalsmeer (see pages 33-4), in
the suburbs of Amsterdam, is
the focus of an annual flower
parade
**October**
The major autumn flower show,
the Herfsttentoonstelling, at the
Bosmuseum
**November**
A Stage Door Festival

*Windmills are now comparatively few and far between since electric power has taken over for pumping out the canals*

church of Amsterdam. The main figure of the procession is Saint Nicholas himself, an elderly and benign gent who is the Dutch equivalent of Santa Claus. With flowing white hair and beard, he rides a white horse along the major roads of the city accompanied by retainers in costume; the venerable saint wears the robes and mitre of a bishop and carries a gilded crozier. Children come in hordes to line the streets.

**Also of note:**
There is an Easter opening of the state rooms of the Royal Palace, and later a summer opening for the months of June, July and August
The market on the Nieuwmarkt, with all sorts of objects both old and not-so-old, is open from mid-May until the end of September
Every Sunday on the Theorbeckeplein there is an open air art market, from mid-March to mid-October
The Rijksmuseum is the place

The big Christmas show in the city is that of Saint Nicholas who presides over a lavish parade in mid-November finishing on the Prins Hendrikkade, appropriately at the St Nicolaas Kerk, the principal Roman Catholic

## SPECIAL EVENTS

for special art exhibitions throughout the year

### HOW TO BE A LOCAL

The Dutch enjoy their own city, and to find them as they are try any 'brown bar' at lunchtimes or in the evenings. Or go into a teashop at any time of day. The Dutch are easy to approach and in Amsterdam (less so in the countryside and small towns perhaps) you will find them affable and easy to talk to. They seem to enjoy meeting English-speaking people. They are naturally helpful and hospitable, and you should in general find it easy to strike up acquaintanceship. By and large the Dutch are free-thinking, so topics of conversation can be varied. The Amsterdammer cycles a lot, both for getting round the city and for exploring the cycle paths around the countryside, and if you too cycle you will not only meet locals, you will be in the press of the traffic with them – they cheerfully aid fellow-bikers. Families will go out cycling or walking at weekends and the atmosphere is usually very cordial. Try taking a picnic and maybe sharing one of the park barbecues that are installed in stopping-places, usually in pretty areas, and as you are all cooking hamburgers or sausages, strike up conversation.

In parks and open spaces the Dutch congregate in summer to picnic and to sit out on the grass. Go to open-air events such as concerts and bandstand performances, or try the theatre. This may be difficult on account of the language, but the audience will be mostly Dutch and there are many things such as ballet, opera and mime shows that have no language barrier. Your interest in things Dutch will be appreciated.

Of course learning a few words of Dutch will help too, although it is a very difficult language to get your tongue around! It is appreciated, however, even if you only learn how to say 'please', 'thankyou' and 'excuse me'.

A good time to meet people and to feel you are taking part in local celebrations is when there are processions or at carnival time (first week of February) when residents are often 'letting their hair down'. There is nothing like a street party for making you feel part of the scene!

Think about trying restaurants off the tourist track – small, unprepossessing places often have local clienteles and are very welcoming.

In an easy, casual, open city like Amsterdam it is hard to offend local people, and relatively easy to get to meet them. Remember that wherever you come from a compliment is always a welcome thing, and locals like to hear their city praised. If you want to find an easy way to break into conversation, just make some pleasing comment about an aspect of the city you particularly enjoy and you will be met with a warm response – and may even strike up a friendship.

*Exploring the canals by pedalo*

## CHILDREN

There is a great deal for
children to do in the city and
its environs. Teenagers will
enjoy visits to places such as
the Melkweg (see page 100) or
the pop concerts in Vondel
Park, or the many special
events set up for younger
visitors to museums and
galleries (usually posted on
gallery notice boards, or ask
the VVV Tourist Office for any
special events that are
current). And remember that
cycling is universal in Holland
and both in the city and the
country the special bike paths
(separate from the main road
and marked with a blue circle
with a cyclist superimposed on
it) are safe, if somewhat
crowded at the rush hour. (See
Bicycles, pages 115-16, for
addresses of rental firms in
Amsterdam). Older children
will enjoy exploring the canals
on their own in a pedalo for
two or four (there are several
rental points, see Canal Boats,
pages 116-19) and they will be
quite safe since the little craft
are not flimsy and most canals
are shallow.
Children will enjoy museum
concerts and the big, brightly
painted street organs that can

## CHILDREN

be found at major central points. These large, unwieldy piped affairs in exotic and even lurid colours, run either by a belt or manually, hammer out Dutch tunes on crowded streets and squares, adding considerably to the atmosphere. One family maintains a tradition that is in danger of dying out, for the organs once common in all European cities, are becoming rare. Holland is now the only country where they can still be seen fairly frequently. There are estimated to be about 60 of them in the country, several having pitches in the centre of Amsterdam. In addition there are smaller organs and instruments played by street musicians, while in summer the big churches usually have organ concerts which can be fascinating, for the organs are ancient instruments – the one in the Nieuwe Kerk beside the Dam dates from 1665, that of the Oude Kerk from 1724. There are 42 historic organs in the churches of the city. An interesting game can be played listening to carillons from the church towers – there are nine carillons in all – comparing and sometimes deciding exactly what time they are calling out. There are guided tours in churches and often a chance to climb the tower – fun for those whose legs are young! Note that Amsterdam has over 40 musical and theatrical performances a day and among them there is bound to be something specially for children.

Simple pastimes such as riding the trams or finding the unusual among the many sculptures of Amsterdam can give much pleasure and children will of course find something of interest in many of the museums listed under What to See, pages 21-32. Worth mentioning in particular is the **Anne Frank House** where children can see the attic room in which the teenage Anne and her family hid from the Germans during World War II and where she wrote her famous diary. See page 26 for details.

There is always the branch of **Madame Tussaud's** to visit.

*Large, loud and luridly coloured street organs hammer out traditional Dutch tunes on busy squares and streets*

Here can be found all sorts of personalities and a section that appeals specially to children – a merry-go-round with caricatures on the horses. Kalverstraat 156. Open daily 10.00 to 18.00; July, August to 19.00.

Amsterdam has its own **Children's Museum** – with a difference! Adults may only go when accompanied by a child! There are lots of possibilities for learning, touching and doing here, and new exhibitions are regularly mounted. The museum is especially meant for the under-12s, but there is something for everyone. There are permanent shows at the neighbouring **Tropenmuseum** which is a museum of peoples of the Third World, innovative

and architecturally exciting with a wide central court, or atrium, and the gallery floors opening onto it with an open, airy effect. Here, cunningly devised, are markets from the Middle East, a street from the West Indies, Bedouin tents and Asian shops along bazaars. It is an intriguing place for anyone, but children will find lots to do here especially on a wet day. 2 Linnaeusstraat, near Mauritskade.

Tropenmuseum open 10.00 to 17.00 Monday – Friday, 12.00 to 17.00 Saturday, Sunday. Children's Museum open specific times school holidays and Sundays. Special programmes Saturday.

Another place loved by children, outside Amsterdam but well worth a day or half-day's outing, is **Madurodam**. This collection of miniature houses set in squares and streets which can be inspected at close quarters is world-famous and very popular and it features all the major monuments of Holland reproduced to scale – very much a children's scale! Detail is microscopic and children will love finding out the tiny aspects of the buildings ranging from church towers to windmills. A trip to Madurodam can be made from mid-March to the end of October, and there are evenings of special illuminations in summer.

You can combine a visit here (there are many coach trips on offer from the cities) with a discovery of The Hague, a compact city with lots to see in this centre of government (see Excursions from Amsterdam, page 61-2).

**Christmas Celebrations** The great day for Amsterdam's children falls usually in mid-November when the much-loved Saint Nicholas arrives by boat in the port of Amsterdam. The Bishop mounts a horse and tours the city, accompanied by his retainers known as the Black Peters, and families all turn out with the children to watch them pass. The costumed assistants throw gingernuts to the children, and there is huge excitement. St Nicholas was Archbishop of Myra in Asia Minor and he lived in the 3rd and 4th centuries AD. His bones repose in Bari in southern Italy, and the cult of St Nicholas spread (probably by sea) as far as Holland where in the medieval era 23 churches were dedicated to him including St Nicholas in Amsterdam. On 5 December Eve (ie 4 December) families gather to give presents and poems to each other, and to

*Merry-go-rounds are perennial favourites*

mark the day of the patron saint of Amsterdam, and of sailors, good old St Nick, or of course, 'Sinterklaas', the delightful old fellow known in so many different guises around the Christian world.

## TIGHT BUDGET

There is plenty of accommodation in cheap hotels and youth hostels in Amsterdam. The VVV Tourist Office at the Centraal Station will help when you arrive. Students can get reductions to museums etc with an International Student Card. You must have proof that you are a full time student and a passport sized photograph. The cheapest tickets for public transport are the strip tickets (stripkaarten) based on a zone system (see pages 120-1). The Museumcard (Museumjaarkart), available from the VVV Tourist Office and museums, gives free admission to 18 museums in Amsterdam as well as many others in the rest of Holland (half-price for under 25's). The Holland Leisure Card, on sale from local tourist offices, lasts for a year. With it visitors can obtain discounts on public transport, excursions, car rental, theatre performances and other useful services. When it comes to eating and drinking, there are of course plenty of cheap restaurants as well as the more expensive ones. Sandwich bars are excellent for light meals and some delicious snacks can be found for sale in some of the markets.

## DIRECTORY

### Arriving

The Netherlands' main international airport is Schiphol, Amsterdam. Several companies run regular car and passenger ferries between Holland and the UK. Many travel companies do package trips to Amsterdam – *Time Off* and *Travelscene* among others. You will need a valid passport (no visa unless staying longer than three months) and a stay of longer than eight days in one place must be reported to the police (this formality, however, is covered by hotel etc registration).

**Rail/Coach Connection** A bus service is run from the airport to KLM's pick-up point at the Centraal Station. It is frequent, about every 15 minutes, takes half an hour. More highly recommended is the train connection between Schiphol and the centre. Trains run about every 15 minutes and are part of the commuter service so not just bound for the airport. You'll need to check the departure boards

*There's many a window like this, with its typical display of porcelain and flowers*

*Bulbs, bulbs and more bulbs!*

and look for trains marked with a small aircraft besides 'Schiphol'. It will take you less than 15 minutes. You may find luggage space is limited and there will be crowds at the rush hours.

### Camping
Local campsites exist near the main Dutch cities and are well equipped and clean with all facilities. The VVV Tourist Office publishes a list of campsites. The only document you will need is your passport. The fee for camping with tent or motorhome is low. The sites in Holland are well run and in addition there are also low price camp-type hostels.

### Car Breakdown
Main highways have frequent patrols by police cars and the ANWB provide mechanical aids and free service to members (an AIT member). The ANWB is listed locally and a call will usually provide swift service for which there will be

a service charge (tel no: 22 44 66).
**Road Services** Assistance tel: 06 08 88 or roadside telephones on major highways.

### Car Rental
Car rental is simple, with all the big agencies represented plus local ones, but, unless you are planning explorations beyond the city, with Amsterdam's chronic parking difficulties a car can just be a nuisance. Rental offices can be found at the airport and in central Amsterdam. You will need an international driver's licence as a rule, and for some companies must be at least 21.

### Chauffeur-driven Cars
Chauffeur-driven cars are available through the VVV Tourist Office with guided tours, if required, and airport pickups.

### Crime
Crime is a problem in the city, since there is a good deal of drug trafficking. Take the usual precautions and do not walk in empty, dark alleys or leave items on car seats where they can be spotted and the car broken into. Women should wear their handbags across their bodies and men keep their wallets in upper pockets.

### Customs Regulations
No visa is necessary for members of the EEC and most other countries but check if you are not in these categories at your Netherlands Embassy before leaving. For customs allowances check with the Dutch Tourist Office in your

*City of canals and cycles: there are bicycles and bicycle parking racks everywhere – and plenty of rental agencies*

locality.

No weapons may be imported into the Netherlands, including knives as well as firearms.

## Doctor/Dentist

See under Pharmacist.

## Domestic Travel

### Bus

Well served with frequent services all over the city on a flat fare basis (see under Transit Authority, below).

### Bicycle

If you are young and energetic then try joining in with the hordes of Amsterdammers who regularly cycle around the city. It is a great way for feeling you are a part of the city as you triumphantly get ahead of stalled traffic in the narrow streets or take a short cut. There are many bike rental agencies and the cost is low but you will need to put down a deposit. This is due to the high incidence of cycle theft in the city, so make sure the bike is secure when parked. You can even take a tour on a bike – *Ena's Bicycle Tour* which lasts 7½ hours! (Information from VVV Tourist office.)

**Rentals** from:

*Rent-a-Bike*, Stationsplein 6. Big and popular.

## DIRECTORY

*Heja*, Bestevaerstraat 39 (tel: 129 211), very cheap.
*Koenders*, Utrechtsedwarsstraat 105 (tel: 248 391), low rates. Bicycles are parked all over the city – racks are everywhere – and the rush hour is a whizz on wheels. With so many bikes there are many pavement repair shops – the machines get a bumping with so many cobbled streets to negotiate. You can also rent mopeds reasonably. Outside the city there are cycle-only routes netting the entire country, the special paths marked with blue-and-white circular markers.

**Paths for cyclists** A round sign of a white cycle on a blue ground indicates paths obligatory for cycles and mopeds. Optional paths are marked with small black signs saying 'fietspad' or 'rijwielpad' and are for cycles but not mopeds. Cycle lanes on main roads are marked with a white cycle on the road surface.

### Canal boats

You can take a water-bus trip, and these are very popular for giving you a feeling of the old aspects of Amsterdam from water level in big, comfortable boats leaving from various points, especially along Damrak and the Rokin. Check the advertising boards for prices and what you get. The boats will usually take you along the 'residential' canals under many low bridges and also give glimpses of the open waters of the Ijsselmeer and the docks beyond the Centraal Station. This is a novel and

*Centraal Station and Stationsplein – a busy place, with the main information centres*

fascinating way to see the city and is certainly recommended. (Dinner cruises tend to be expensive and not a bargain.) The VVV Tourist Office at the main station has detailed schedules and prices of boat trips.

*Canal boat companies and departure points*
*Rederij d'Amstel*, Nicolaas Witsenkade opposite Heineken Brewery (tel: 265 636)

*Holland Int. Rondvaart*, opposite Central Station (tel: 227 788)

*Rederij P Kooy BV*, Rokin by Spui (tel: 233 810)

*Rederij Lovers BV*, Prins Hendrikkade opposite number 76 (tel: 222 181)

*Meyers Rondvaarten*, Damrak jetty 4–5 (tel: 234 208)

*Rederij Noord-Zuid*, Stadhouderskade opposite Parkhotel (tel: 791 370)

*Rederij Plas CV*, jetty 1–3 (tel: 245 406

**Museumboat** In addition to the popular Touristram there is an allied boat service – the Museumboat, running on a schedule to the various points at which you can get off and visit one of the city's many museums. After your visit catch the boat again on to the next museum.

**Special boat tours** Some boats will make special tours to include pub visits, a tour of a diamond factory, even a theatre visit, but in general these are better arranged separately for yourself.
Though it is true to say that in central Amsterdam you are

never more than a few yards from a waterway. There is a useful publication obtainable from tourist offices in Holland and abroad called *Cruises in Amsterdam* that gives detailed information and times and charges. Some cruises are 90 minutes, some as long as two hours. Most boats operate from April until the end of October; during this time the canals are illuminated each night, while in the winter they are lit up two or three times a week. Church spires, house-fronts, bridges glow with lights giving a different and romantic aspect that negates the somewhat banal explanations given by the guide, or in some cases, the tape.

*The Damrak, leading into The Dam, at the heart of the city*

**Canal boating on your own** If you want to be adventurous then try a canal boat tour on your own – it is quite possible and consists of renting a pedal boat for two or four persons. It is a good way of seeing the little backwaters where the big boats don't ply. Expect to pay a deposit. *Canal Bike* has several moorings, so you can go from one and leave the pedal-boat at another; *Roell* has only one near the Amstel Hotel (Mauritskade). Summer operation only, and the little rectangular craft are solid and safe.

*Roell*: Mauritskade 1 (tel: 929 124)
*Canal Bike*: Five locations, including Centraal Station (tel: 265 574)
Most companies will of course

do group rentals for large boats, and also offer motorboats and 'family' boats. The large cruise boats have lavatories on board.

### Cars
Drivers bringing in a car or other vehicle must produce registration certificate, proof of insurance in EEC countries (a 'green card', or temporary insurance cover obtained at the border crossing), also an international identity disc affixed to the rear. Trailers and caravans must be 'used' or else a registration certificate produced.

**Speed** A general speed limit in built up areas of 50km per hour (31mph); in residential areas marked with a white house on a blue background

cars should drive at a walking pace. General speed limit outside built up areas, 80km per hour (50mph). On highways and motorways, 120km per hour (75mph).

### Coach Tours
A number of special tours are available in Amsterdam giving you a good but rather isolated introduction to a city that really needs closer contact than the wide windows of a tourist bus. See the VVV for information on all kinds of tours not only of Amsterdam but of its nearby villages and other Dutch towns for half or full day explorations at reasonable rates, some with meals and token drinks included. The commentary is usually by a professional guide, but tapes are also used.

### Metro
A new service of two major lines, which is often being extended, and will no doubt have more lines added in the 1990s. It serves central Amsterdam and works on the same fare basis as the trams and the buses, but is usually of little use to the tourist since it principally serves commuters coming in from the Amsterdam suburbs.

### Trains
Centraal Station is of course a busy place with over 1,000 trains arriving and departing from the suburbs and principal European centres. It is a useful place for departures to other cities around Amsterdam (see Excursions from Amsterdam pages 55-62). There is an information desk within the

## DIRECTORY

station providing all necessary facts about local travel.

### Trams

There are 13 city lines and the big, wide trams can be seen all over the city. Bus and tram shelters have maps of the system encompassing the whole city, but unless you have friends or relations in the suburbs it is unlikely that you will need to go far afield. To understand the fare system, see below, Transit Authority.

### Transit Authority/GVB

Centraal Station is a place you will not be able to avoid! It is surrounded by many useful services, a web of tramlines, and numerous stops that have all been updated to give electronic information. Here also is the home of the Amsterdam Transit Authority, or GVB.

The GVB can supply you with all the information and requirements for getting about

*Several central streets are for pedestrians only, for instance Kalverstraat (above)*

Amsterdam on public transport. It controls all bus and tram services as well as the two Metro lines. Pick up a map, information folder and as many free brochures as you need.

**Buying a ticket** There are several kinds of tickets – you can use the basic single flat fare ticket purchased from the bus or tram driver, or you can get one-, two- and three-day tickets at set prices. The strip tickets (or *stripkaarten*) are cheapest but need some understanding since they are based on a zone system and you will need to know how many zones you are crossing before stamping them in the machine. (The city has 11 zones, but for many tourists transport within the main central zone is all that is needed.) The strip tickets are purchased in tens (or 15 at a more economic rate at the GVB or at post offices) and they are then valid for an hour's travel and include transfers to other lines and the Metro. Inspectors can fine you on the spot if you do not hold a valid time-stamped ticket.

**Times of services** Most of the bus and tram services start early in the morning and so does the Metro. They will go on until midnight, or after, when a night bus service begins (the GVB will also provide you with a Night Service brochure). You can either pay the flat fare, or use a strip ticket.

## Taxis

Taxis carry a lighted sign on the roof when free and are hired as a rule from a taxi stand. (They do not always respond to being hailed.) They are metered except for journeys beyond the central area and into the country. (Schiphol counts as out of town and the fare will be from 40 to 50 Fl.) Tips are included in the metered fare, but are topped up by rounding the charge to the next guilder as a rule. Central taxi telephone number: 77 77 77.

**Touristram** Operated by the VVV (see below), this service runs regularly. Most cities have special bus services for tourists, but Amsterdam operates one of her famous trams. For details and fares (it can be linked with Museumboat trip) check at the VVV Tourist Office.

## Walking

This is the best way to see Amsterdam, and of course the cheapest, with shoe leather being your only concern. So pack a comfortable pair of shoes and also a warm casual outfit with a scarf and a folding umbrella (rain is common in Holland most of the autumn and winter) and set off. You do not have to have a map but it is handy and by day there is almost nowhere you cannot go safely. (Two suggested routes are included in this book, on pages 46-55.) You will find that several central streets are for walkers only, notably the central shopping streets of Kalverstraat and Nieuwendijk which snake through the middle of the city. Do not make the mistake of confusing cycle paths with footpaths in some of the more recently developed areas because the two-wheelers, often with an extra passenger on the back, can hurtle along at high speed and at night lights are a rarity so you do not always see cyclists coming! Walks planned with care can always end at a bus or tram stop and you can ride back home. You are not likely to get lost either, because the U-shaped plan of central Amsterdam means that in quick time you will cross a canal and find where you are, and the streets, despite often long and unwieldy names almost impossible to pronounce for the non-Dutch speaker, are well marked on the corners with neat blue and white markers. In addition a new sign has been appearing

# DIRECTORY

*No excuse needed to stop off for an ice cream – like all Dutch dairy products, it is rich, creamy and delicious*

on Amsterdam's streets, a series of pointers attached to lamp-posts and showing clearly on their orange and grey rectangular shapes the directions of tourist attractions. There are guided tours of the city on offer, walking with a group leader who is usually a registered guide.

Like any city, Amsterdam constantly changes, so check for latest information on new routes at the VVV. **The VVV Tourist Office** is at Stationsplein 10, opposite the station, telephone 26 64 44. Correspondence to PO Box 3901, 10001, AS Amsterdam. There is also a service point at the other end of the old town at Leidsestraat 106, by the Leidseplein.

**Electricity**
220 volts. Two round pins.

**Embassies and Consulates**
Great Britain: Koningslaan 44 (tel: 764343) (Consulate)
USA: Museumplein 19 (tel: 790321) (Consulate)

**Emergency Telephone Numbers**
Police 222222
Fire brigade 212121
Ambulance 5 55 5555
SOS Doctor 642111
SOS Dentist 79 18 21

**Entertainment Information**
There are numerous posters and notice boards around the Leidseplein and in theatres and cabarets. Hotel porters have leaflets. The VVV Tourist Office has information on events and the local newspapers carry advertisements. Look for free sheets listing current attractions at the VVV and newstands.

**Holidays – Public and Religious**
New Year's Day
Good Friday
Easter Sunday and Monday
Queen's Birthday (30 April)
Ascension Day
Whit Sunday and Monday
Christmas Day
Boxing Day

**Lost Property**
Waterlooplein 11 (tel: 559 80 05) *Open*: Monday to Friday 12.00 to 15.00.

## Medical Care

Foreign visitors have the right to medical assistance in accordance with the Dutch health service law. Those originating from within the EEC (Common Market Countries) will need an insurance form which can be obtained before leaving home – ask your doctor or DHSS office for the relevant form (E110, E111, or E112). If in need of medical assistance you may find you have to pay directly and then claim costs back from the National Health Service on return, so be sure to obtain receipts.

No vaccinations are required.

## Money

There are no import and export restrictions regarding foreign exchange for non-residents. Money can be changed at the official GWK offices at airports, stations and at border points. Besides cash you can also change travellers' cheques, and credit card transactions for cash. Money can also be exchanged at banks and at post offices and at certain VVV Tourist Offices. Commissions can vary widely, so look around at the various possibilities especially if exchanging large sums.

The money system is based on the *guilder* (also called a *florin*) and cents (one hundred to the guilder). In actual fact the smallest coin is now a five cent piece.

Credit cards are accepted everywhere in Amsterdam for sales in restaurants, hotels, shops, and at stations for tickets for trains or at airports for air tickets. Car rental agencies also accept leading credit cards, and the main ones (American Express, Diners Club, Eurocard and Visa) all have principal offices in the country.

## Opening Times

### Banks

Open from 09.00 to 16.00/17.00 and sometimes later on Thursday and Friday late-night shopping evenings.

### Shops

Mondays–Fridays 08.30/09.00 to 17.30/18.00; Saturdays shops close 16.00/17.00. Shops have individual closing days or half days, indicated by signs. Late-night shopping on Thursdays and Fridays.

### Museums

Usually open from 10.00. Usually closed Mondays.

### Pharmacists

Doctor, Dentist, 24-hour doctor service (tel: 642111). 24-hour Tourist Medical Service, Jacob Obrechtstraat 67 (tel: 737567).

## Places of Worship

For foreign language services and times of local ones ask at the VVV Tourist Office.

## Police

In Amsterdam the police have a special alarm number: 222222
The Main office is at Elandsgracht 117, 1016 TT (tel: 5 599111)

## Post Office

The Main Post Office on Nieuwezijds Voorburgwal (no 182) is open every weekday from 08.30. Saturdays from 09.00. Closed Sundays. A remarkable building in a palatial 19th-century style. Letters can be received here and held for pick up (Poste Restante). Post boxes have two slots, one for local and one for abroad. To post parcels use the Post Office at the Oosterdokskade, same hours as the Main Post Office.

### Telephone
International calls can be made from phone boxes or from post offices by dialling 09 and, when tone changes, the international code. Calls from hotels are more expensive.

### Time difference
Central European Time Zone (so most of the year Amsterdam is one hour ahead of London, five hours ahead of New York).

### Tips
Almost always included in hotel and restaurant bills, you can add a little extra for good service if you wish. Taxi meters include a tip, although it is customary to round up fares to the nearest guilder.

### Toilets
As always, easier for men than women but they are not plentiful in the city and the best way is to use hotels or cafés where you can usually find adequate and clean facilities (but be sure to keep small coins in hand for tips for attendants).

### Tourist Offices
**GVB**
Local city and transport

information booth on the Stationsplein.
Open every day (tel: [08.00 to 23.00] 272727

### VVV Tourist Office
Information from the Stationsplein office open year round, every day including Sundays (tel: 26 64 44) Address for advance information: PO Box 3901, 10001 AS Amsterdam, Netherlands

## LANGUAGE

The Dutch will deem it a compliment if you try to speak their language, but be prepared for smiles and merriment at your mispronunciations unless you happen to be good at reproducing the glottal, guttural sounds that make up the Dutch language. Descended from Germanic tongues and affected by both Saxon and Frisian invaders, it seems impossibly complicated at times. And as over 70 per cent of the Dutch seem to speak English, often surprisingly fluently, you can get quite lazy even if you are determined to try the language. Still, the following words and phrases are useful:
**yes** ja
**no** nee
**please** alstublieft
**thankyou** dank u, or dank u wel
**hello** dag
**good morning/afternoon/evening** goede morgen/middag/avond
**are you well?** hoe gaat het met u?
**very well** uitstekend

**pardon me/excuse me** pardon
**I come from England/USA**
Ik kom uit England/USA
**breakfast** ontbijt
**dinner** diner
**sandwich** broodje
**cup of coffee/tea**
kopje koffie/thee
**dish of the day** daschotel
**may I order?**
mag ik even bestellen?
**how much does this cost?**
wat kost dit?
**may I pay?**
mag ik even afrekenen?
**inclusive of VAT and
service charge**
inclusief BTW en bedieningsgeld
**open** open
**closed** gesloten
**no entry** verboden toegang
**a ticket to . . .**
een kaartje naar . . .
**one-way ticket** enkele reis
**return** retour
**where's the . . .** waar is het? . . .
**post office** loket
**chemist** apotheek
**hospital** ziekenhuis
**doctor** dokter
**station** station
**bank** bank
**postcard** briefkaart
**letter box** brievenbus
**telephone booth** telefooncel

**one** een
**two** twee
**three** drie
**four** vier
**five** vijf
**six** zes
**seven** zeven
**eight** acht
**nine** negen
**ten** tien

To try to speak Dutch you will
need a dictionary and a
pronunciation guide. There are

*The hungry tourist is spoiled for
choice with the wide range of
cuisine, at a wide range of prices,
that Amsterdam has on offer*

a few basic rules that may help
with pronunciation:

ee is pronounced 'ay'
g on its own is a guttural sound
almost like an h
j is normally soft as in 'yah' for
ja (yes) or else not sounded at
all as when it precedes a k
oo is usually shorter than it
appears to make the sound
'oh'. Ij is pronounced 'eye'.

Dutch has similar roots to
Flemish and also German, so
you will find that most Dutch
people have some knowledge
of both languages as well as
French. To begin with, try to
master words and short
phrases until you can manage
the curious guttural glottal
sounds of many of the words,
some of which can be
dauntingly long!

## ACKNOWLEDGEMENTS

The Automobile Association would like to thank the following photographers and libraries for their assistance in the compilation of this book.

INTERNATIONAL PHOTOBANK 8/9 waterbus & canal, 36 Montelbaanstoren, 42/3 Skinny Bridge, 115 bicycles.

NATURE PHOTOGRAPHERS LTD 63 black tailed godwit (T Andrewartha), 64/5 sea holly, 75 pool frog (P R Sterry), 67 yellow horned poppy (R Tidman), 68/9 Bewick swan, 70 Friesland (C & J Knights), 72/3 bittern (J Wilson).

CHRISTINE OSBORNE PICTURES 7 eel fisherman, 10/11 buildings, 13 transport, 23 van Gogh Museum, 24/5 Historisch Museum, 26/7 Joods Historisch Museum, 30/1 *Wheatfield*, van Gogh Museum, 33 Willet-Holthuysen Museum, 34 Singel flower market, 39 New Church, 40 Red Light District, 44 clogs, 46/7 canal houses, 53 Westerkerk, 54 Alkmaar cheese market, 56 Delft porcelain factory, 61 tulips, 77 Schiphol airport, 78/9 Dutch cheeses, 80 antique shop, 82 flea market, 83 shopping for diamonds, 85 smoked eels, 86/7 Indonesian food, 88 café society, 90/1 Indonesian restaurant, 93 accommodation, 94 The American Hotel, 99 night lights, 100/1 Stadsschouwburg theatre, 102/3 café, 104 womens' gay bar, 105 tulips, 106/7 windmill, 109 pedalos on the canal, 112 merry-go-round, 113 window, 116/7 Centraal Station, 118/9 shops, 120 Kalvestraat, 122 ice cream, 125 menu.

SPECTRUM COLOUR LIBRARY Cover: Keizersgracht, 14/5 doorway, 16/7 houses & café, 18 house front, 28 stained glass window, 51 Rembrandtsplein, 96/7 Doelen Crest Hotel, 100/1 street organ, 114 bulb market.

ZEFA PICTURE LIBRARY (UK) LTD 4 Amsterdam, 21 Rijksmuseum.

### Author's acknowledgements

The author is indebted to both Marcel Balthus at the Netherlands Board of Tourism and Travelscene for assistance in the preparation of this book.